W9-CTD-559

PEARL'S
KITCHEN

ALSO BY PEARL BAILEY
The Raw Pearl
Talking to Myself

PEARL'S KITCHEN

An Extraordinary Cookbook
by Pearl Bailey

HARCOURT BRACE JOVANOVICH
NEW YORK AND LONDON

Printed in the United States of America

Library of Congress Cataloging in Publication Data
Bailey, Pearl.
    Pearl's kitchen.
    1. Cookery.   2. Bailey, Pearl.   I. Title.
TX715.B158   641.5   73–6624
ISBN 0–15–171600–5

B C D E

To Humanity
who has so surrounded
me with "Love" — my cup
runneth over —
Love returned
Pearl

Contents

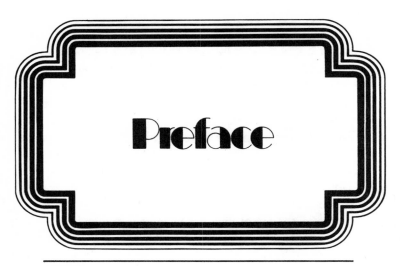

Preface

T IS ALMOST two in the morning and I am sitting at my kitchen table alone. The neighborhood is asleep and my own house is silent except for the radio across the room, which plays music, just soft and low. I have a very strong feeling, deep, that I am altogether at home here. Ever since my childhood the kitchen has been a special place for me—I started learning to cook at Mama's stove in Philadelphia when I was eight years old. Since then, my life has been joyously busy with vaudeville, cabarets, theater, and television. I have traveled the world. I have seen hardship and comparative wealth. I have visited the famous places and have touched at one time or another a great many of the famous and glamorous people in this world. Yet, through all the years, I have always come back to my kitchen, wherever it happened to be, in order to find peace and the special warmth of the heart and hearth.

At night like this when my husband and children are asleep, and my dogs have fallen to silence for lack of anything more to grumble and bark at, I find myself drawn to the kitchen to cook a bit, write a bit about my thoughts of the day and meditate upon their meaning. I communicate with my life and with God.

Sitting here thinking of yesterday and cooking for tomorrow, I have written this book. It is a cookbook, but not a typical one. I'll tell you how to make some wonderful dishes all right, but I don't want to do just that and nothing more. While I am telling you *what* I cook and approximately *how* I do it, I want to try to communicate *why* I cook. Practically speaking I don't have to cook at all. I could make arrangements to have all of that done for us. I cook because emotionally it is necessary for me to cook, and I want to explore this mystical satisfaction, this meaning and joy that comes from my activities in the kitchen.

I said that I could tell you *approximately* how I cook because I want to warn you that I am not always good at giving you precise quantities. In fact, I doubt very much that I cook the same dish exactly the same way twice in a row. That is another way that my book differs from a regular cookbook. Then too, my cooking tends very strongly toward simplicity and economy. Gourmet cooking is not my way, as you will see. I will be talking about regular everyday meals that ordinary human beings can cook over and over again. I am fond of honest food well prepared so that the family can respond to it day after day. Just for spice, I will throw in some recipes by my friends, and some of those may get a bit more fancy.

The idea for this book and the motive to write it came to me when I lived on a ranch in 1958. I had a very large kitchen then and I did a lot of cooking. One day when I was tasting and talking to myself and telling myself how this dish and that dish tasted and what I remembered about times in the past when I had cooked it before, I decided that I ought to write some of these things down. I put a notebook in the kitchen and began to jot things down once in a while. In the beginning, I felt obligated to be more precise about the recipes than I am when I am cooking them myself. That, of course, was useless. The fact is that it takes more than ingredients and technique to cook a good meal. A good cook puts something of *himself* into the preparation—he cooks with enjoyment, anticipation, spontaneity, and he is willing to experiment.

Cooking is like living—we can tell other people, perhaps our children, what we would have them do in their lives, and yet when it comes down to it they have to live for themselves. If my recipes do not suit you fully, then please take pleasure in experimenting with them. Live with them and put yourself into them until you become fully satisfied. Satisfy yourself, but don't cook selfishly. To cook is to share, and it is as important to me as walking onto the stage to full applause. Cooking is as crucial as anything I do in life, because I like to see the smiles on people's faces when they enjoy something I have prepared. I cook as I live.

The kitchen is the center of activity in my house and it is the center of my silence on nights like this. It is the room where the forms of living seem to start and end; it is the room where I make sense of life, birth, death, work, play, hurt, and joy. With this book I reach out for an audience of people who love to live simply, people who understand about the mystical side of cooking, people who could join me happily in a good solid one-pot meal, a full three-course dinner, or just a plain cup of good coffee.

PEARL'S
KITCHEN

Mama looking over My Shoulder

AMA'S KITCHEN, the one I remember, was in Philadelphia, where I did most of my growing up. Mama, who was a handsome woman with deep dimples in her cheeks, kept our house spotlessly clean. It was a real thing with her to have everything polished and shiny all the time. Papa was a hod carrier during the week, and on Sunday he was a Reverend at the House of Prayer. My brother and my sisters and I were not allowed into Mama's kitchen very much. In fact, she didn't like to have company in there at all, but she would let us in when she was going to teach us something. Mama was a fast cook and a good one. She had a way of preparing those simple dishes so that the very aroma floating through the house could make our little mouths water. It meant everything to Mama just knowing that we liked the things she prepared at mealtime. It was there with Mama standing behind me that I had my first experiences with cooking. I learned mostly by watching rather than by doing because Mama was very much in command in her own kitchen and she wasn't about to have her children messing something up for her. For her, cooking was an expression of love, and serving at the table was an experience in sharing her affection with us all.

Sunday mornings remain particularly vivid in my memory. Papa always gave us a certain amount of

3

religion at the table, but on Sunday morning, since he was the Reverend, we really got it. First, we had grace. Then came Papa's speech on good behavior. Then came the Twenty-third Psalm, possibly followed by three chapters from Daniel, nine from Isaiah, and some from a few other spots in the Bible. All this had to do with living right and behaving yourself. We sat quietly and listened but our little mouths were becoming drizzly and our eyes were popping out as we looked over toward the stove.

On that stove every Sunday morning was Mama's fried chicken. Mama could cook the best fried chicken in the world. Now most people think that the tradition is to have fried chicken for dinner on Sunday. Mama did it the other way. She would get up and go down to Ridge Avenue to get her chicken killed that same morning. Then come back and fry them up. She had a way of putting everything in that big skillet at once and then just moving it around so that in about twenty or twenty-five minutes everything was perfectly done. It was a real technique, and to tell you the truth, I can't really do it yet. I loved all of that chicken, but my very favorite part was wings. I could have eaten dozens of wings. I liked the necks too, and sometimes the gizzard. Somehow, the so-called better part of the chicken seemed too rich or too filling for me. It reminds me that there was an old wives' tale that said that if you ate the chicken gizzard you would become pretty. Everyone at our table certainly made a big deal about who got to eat the chicken gizzard. Now I ask you, what could there be in a chicken gizzard that would make you pretty?

I wish I could tell you how Mama fried that chicken. The best I can do is give you as much as I remember. First of all, I guess it would help to get chickens absolutely fresh. By the way, I'll tell you a story about that later. She would salt and pepper the chicken and sprinkle it with flour and then throw that boy in the skillet and cover the top. Once in a while she would take the top off and turn some pieces over and put the top back on again. Mama cooked in lard, but to make it extra special, she would put one stick of butter in there with the lard. Now I've tried it since and I can't do *one* chicken that way, much less three or four in the same pan the way Mama did. It had that wonderful brown crispness on the outside, but inside it was moist, so nice that three or four days later it would still be moist inside, but cooked well to the bone. Now, believe me, that's important to me. I absolutely can't stand to bite into a piece of chicken or fish and find it the least bit on the undercooked side.

As I said, Mama insisted on having her chickens killed fresh every Sunday morning. Recently, I passed by the place on Ridge Avenue where Mama got chickens and it is still there. I guessed they passed it from father to son. Well anyway, Mama was kosher all the way; that chicken had to be fresh. One particular morning she couldn't get there for one reason or another so she sent me. Now I have to tell you that I like birds in their proper places, but I am not too much for being up close to birds and I certainly don't enjoy going where the people have birds flying loose in the house. They can be beautiful but I just don't prefer them up close. As a matter of fact, I think it is unkind to confine any animal to a place other than his habitat. Anyway, that has nothing to do with my feelings about birds and particularly live chickens. When she sent me to Ridge Avenue, Mama said to me, "Blow those feathers back, feel his breast." Ho! ho! ho! Blow the feathers back! I wasn't about to do that. As a matter of fact, I was scared to death the chicken would peck me. I went into the store and told the man, "Not fat, but a nice plump chicken," and then I backed up into the corner and waited. The man blew the feathers back and I guess that made it easier to tell Mama a little white lie when I got home. I never went near the bird. Sure enough, when I got back to our house and stepped inside, the first thing Mama asked was "Did you blow those feathers back?" Now I disliked lying very much but I told Mama a little lie. I figured, after all, didn't I see the man blow the feathers back?

Mama always had one of us kids set the table.

Funny thing is, I still remember that she would say, "Now don't set a plate for me." One time I said, "Mama, how's that? Why not?" She said the same thing she always said, "I'll just have a little saucer on the corner of the table, one like you put under the cup." Then when it came mealtime, Mama would sit at the corner of the table with her little saucer. Once in a while she would ask someone to put a little fat in the saucer for Mama and she would eat that.

At first when I noticed this I worried about it. I thought, "Now Mama is not eating. Something must be wrong—I wonder what's wrong with Mama." On the other hand, after a while I noticed that Mama was getting larger and larger. Number one, she did a pretty good job with that little saucer at the corner of the table. Without our thinking of it, she really consumed as much as all the kids put together, bless her heart. But that was not the whole story about how Mama started to get large.

Years ago, just like today, people used to play at numbers. The policy, illegal or not, and my Mama loved to play her numbers. She would go out in the morning to play them. Somebody would say to her, "Mama, aren't you going to have some breakfast?" She'd say, "No, not a thing." Then she would almost seem to get angry, or maybe just very tough. We knew we shouldn't mention it any more. Then she would pick up her little policy slip —about fifty or seventy-five cents' worth—and head out the door.

I remember she would play a straight number and then she would work some kind of combination which was called a bolita. It had something to do with the end numbers. Mama had all sorts of ways of picking her numbers. She would count things in her dreams and then she would spend some time in her daydreams figuring out what she would do if she won. But I guess she never did.

Anyway, one day Mama tore out of the house at breakfast time and by mistake she left one of her number slips on the table. Well, little Pearlie Mae saw that and picked it up and tore out behind her. Mama had a real head start on me, so I was hurrying down Norris Street trying to catch up. Along the way I happened to pass a restaurant with a big plate-glass window. First I passed it by and then something struck me—I took a couple of skips backward and stuck my face up against the window. There sat my wonderful Mama, pancakes stacked as high as her head, sausage on a plate next to them, and there were home-fried potatoes and coffee. Mama had her head buried down eating away. So, naturally, I tapped on the window and smiled. I thought she could read my lips so I mouthed, "Mama, you left one of your number slips," and I held it up. Mama looked up, but she didn't smile. Those big beautiful dimples were not showing. When she really smiled those dimples must have been two inches deep. She waved her hand at me to come in, but sternly. I really couldn't figure out what was going on.

When I got inside I handed her the slip and I was going to sit down. She said, "Now go on back home." So I did. Later on, when Mama got home she said, "It's a terrible thing when a Mother has to have her own children come spying on her." She was really burned up and embarrassed, because now I knew why she was tearing out so early in the morning and now I knew why Mama was swelling up that way. I never had a chance to catch her any more (not that I looked for her, because I knew better). Frankly, I am just sure she changed restaurants.

Going out to the restaurant and to place her policy slip each morning was about the only time Mama left the house. She stayed right there at Twenty-third and Norris, or within a few blocks of there, for thirty years. I don't think she ever went into a neighbor's house, as far as I can remember. Mama stayed in her house, which really was her castle, and she ran it efficiently and with great dedication. Even though she had very little money to work with, she did a splendid job. Now I find I am the same way. I like my neighbors and I think that they like me—we speak and we bow, but we do not get involved in each other's affairs. I know that if my neighbors really need me, I will help them and that they will help me, but we pay very little attention to neighborhood business. That is not my bag.

Naturally, we loved Mama very dearly. Nevertheless, on occasion we did things that really got her peeved at us. Don't forget, she liked her house clean, and she didn't like to have company fooling around in the kitchen making her burn her food. Sometimes, like many mothers, she would have that ill scene. If she got angry at one of us, she would sometimes tell us together, "I won't be here long, because I haven't been feeling well lately." We would ask, "What's the matter, Mama?" She would answer, "Oh, nothing. God is good, He'll take me away and give me peace." Right away all our little faces got so sad. Actually I think there was never anything really wrong, but Mamas have that effect on you. She used to have an expression when she would get peeved at us: "I've been down in the Valley of the Shadow of Death for you."

Now I said that Mama didn't have a lot of extra money to work with. She had to keep an eye on her bills. The telephone bill used to drive her crazy, particularly when some of the children were old enough to be away and calling home long distance. If Mama got a phone bill over five dollars, she would really scream. My brother, Willie, used to call home collect all the time, working or not. You see, Willie, being the only boy, was pretty much spoiled by Mama when he was little. He would call and the operator would tell Mama it was from Willie, collect. Mama finally started to say on these occasions "Mrs. Bailey doesn't live here." Actually, by this time she and Papa had separated and Mama had remarried, so she was really Mrs. Robinson. She wasn't telling a lie. Then Willie would start screaming and say "Mama, it's me," shouting right over the operator, and sometimes Mama would just hang up.

I really don't think she was being mean, she just wasn't going to pay those high phone bills.

Willie wasn't the only offender—as time went on the rest of us would take a notion to call Mama sometimes more often than we really needed to. I never did call collect myself because I have always had a very special feeling about paying my own way. Mama would take my calls. One time I tried to call home and I couldn't even find the listing, the number had been changed and they had nothing in Mama's name. Later on, when I got there, I told her about the problem and finally she told me what she had done. In her own quiet and efficient way, Mama had solved the problem. She had canceled her phone and had a new one listed in the name of Safronia Bailey. Safronia, you may be interested to know, was our cat.

I guess Mama was not always a great cook, and I really don't know where she learned the art of the kitchen. Years after I left home, Papa told me a story about the first chicken Mama tried to cook. Soon after they were married, he suggested that Mama try to cook the chicken. Well, she cooked it all right. She just killed it and plucked it and put it in the oven, insides and all. I have told you as much as I can remember about the way Mama worked magic with chicken after she learned how it was done. While I am on the subject of her wonderful cooking, I would like to pass along some of the recipes that I remember best from my childhood.

CORN ON THE COB, MAMA-STYLE

In some sense, most of what I know about cooking is Mama-style. That's where I learned most of what I know. I don't have any fancy recipes because Mama didn't have any. Whatever fancy dishes I put in this book will be those that have been given to me by friends. I am not a gourmet chick, so that's it. I leave that to other people.

You wouldn't think there would be much you could do about preparing corn on the cob to make it special, but Mama did it.

Put water in the pot, but not enough to cover the corn, and bring the water to a boil. Lay the corn in there. Add 2 or 3 tablespoons of sugar, a bit more if you like. Now add a little milk, fresh or evaporated. Put the top on. In just a very few minutes, that corn will be tender and delicious. You will learn how long to leave it so it will be just the way you like it best. Take it out and sprinkle on a little salt and pepper. A little butter may help, but it is really not necessary if you cook it the way Mama did.

CORN AND TOMATOES

Whether you use fresh corn or canned corn is up to you. Fresh is the best, and if it happens to be left over on the cob from yesterday, that doesn't hurt a thing. Mama would put everything in the same pot—corn and tomatoes (also either canned or fresh), bacon grease or a piece of fatback, salt and pepper. Once she had everything in the pot, she added water, just enough to cover, and let everything boil with the top on. Sometimes she fried the bacon or fatback first, then poured the grease into the pot while it was boiling. When she got around to tasting it, as often as not, she would add a dash of sugar until she had it just the way she wanted it. Then she let it boil a while longer and finally would take the top off the pot and let it simmer down a bit. She then thickened the mixture with flour just before she took it off the fire. Now I don't know how this sounds to you, but it makes my mouth water just thinking about Mama's corn and tomatoes. She would put that on the table with a piece of some kind of meat and possibly a bowl of collard greens or string beans. Dinner delicious! If you ever decide to serve it just this way, the best of your guests will appreciate your exquisite taste.

CHITLINGS

The very idea of chitlings turns up many a nose. Usually, you will notice that those are the people who say "chitterlings" and they don't really know what they are talking about anyway. Chitlings, that's the intestines of pigs, can really be very, very good. One of the things that turns most people off a bit is that sometimes they don't smell all that great while they are cooking. I don't care too much for that odor myself, but I do love chitlings. One of the things that Mama would tell you if she were here is to be sure that you start off by washing them clean, then turn them inside out and pull a lot of the fat out of them. At this point, you are probably beginning to think that you didn't have the right thing in mind after all. Don't confuse chitlings with tripe. Tripe is the lining of the stomach, and it is kind of spongy like. But chitlings you turn inside out. I wouldn't even try for tripe in my book because I think it is pretty difficult to cook it right. The Italians have it down pretty close. Oh, I saw tripe all right as a little girl at the market and I wanted to taste it. I used to see it on the counter where the meat and fish were. I wondered what that thing was with the little squares in it. It always looked like a bunch of little honeycombs to me and I really wanted to taste it. When I finally did taste it, I was a grown woman. I ordered it at a wonderful Italian restaurant in New York, Amalfi's.

Anyway, back to chitlings. After you have cleaned them well, you put them in a lot of water (about ¾ pot) and boil them down for a good long time until they are just tender. A lot of people eat them just like that with salt and pepper. Some people put vinegar on them and they are delicious that way; and some people do the very best thing of all, they take them out of the pot and coat them with flour, put them in hot bacon grease and fry them. That's my favorite way to eat chitlings. For anyone who hasn't experienced this delight, the main problem is to get over thinking about what chitlings are in the beginning.

HOG'S HEAD

Chitlings made me think of the tradition of cooking a hog's head or hog's jaw as a kind of ritual on New Year's Eve. It certainly was a popular thing to do in my neighborhood in those days. They took the whole head of the hog most of the time. Yes, the teeth were there and yes, the nose was there, and you might think that would look pretty ugly. Yes, but it tasted good. Anyway, when it is New Year's Eve, if you have had a little bit of something to drink it looks a little better, better still if you've had a lot to drink.

When you are about to cook a hog's head, you have to put it down in about ¾ pot of water and cook it like you would pig's feet—a very long time. Don't forget, a hog's head is about as hard as some people's heads. So you start that first, then later you put on your black-eyed peas. I tell how to do that elsewhere in the book.

By the way, don't get hog jaw mixed up with hog *maw*. The maw is the stomach and that's not what we are talking about now. Toward the end it might be a good idea to put on some rice and then you could have Hopping John. Hopping John is nothing more than black-eyed peas put over some steamed rice. It is simple but absolutely delicious, and it is a special for New Year's Eve.

This ritual makes me think of some of the superstitions involved with New Year's Day. One that I remember said that it was bad luck if a woman came to your door first on New Year's Day. Some of the older people in the neighborhood used to send one of the boys out early in the morning on some kind of errand so that he would be sure to return and come through the front door before some woman arrived. Now between you and me, I know some broads who could come to my door at any time on any day of the year and bring bad luck. They walk up the driveway, rap on the door, and want to talk about things that are none of their business. A complete waste of time.

Mama took in roomers once in a while, but just one at a time. She was very particular about whom she had in her house. For one thing, she wanted the rooms kept very clean and for another thing she ordinarily didn't like to have a roomer who wanted to use the kitchen because that was Mama's place. One time though she had a very nice young man in the house whose name was Henry, from South Carolina. Henry had his room and he also had the privilege of using the kitchen once in a while.

RICE HENRY

It turned out that Henry was a very, very good cook, and I learned a few things from him. Hopping John made me think about this because it really is important that you know how to cook rice properly. Henry could do it. I still can't do it as well as he could, but I can pass along some of his technique to you. First of all, you have to wash rice very, very thoroughly—rinse it 2 or 3 times and keep pouring off that whitish fluid. I put the rice in the pot so that the water is about 2 inches over the rice and let it boil for 5 to 7 minutes. By this time, the water is getting low enough to almost touch the top of the rice. Then turn off the fire and put a top or a plate or a piece of aluminum foil over the pan and just let it steam there. Some people get pretty fancy and use a double boiler for this. I did that at first, but I have found it is not necessary. It works perfectly well the way Henry did it. That rice will be as beautiful as it is in the best Japanese or Chinese restaurants.

One thing you may not realize is that rice really is good for you. I know when I was in the hospital most recently with a heart problem they gave me quite a bit of rice. I am no dietician, but I know that it is possible to live almost on rice alone. It is nearly sufficient, so put more rice in your diet. It is nutritious and filling, and it is reasonable for your pocketbook and heart.

OKRA HENRY

Henry cooked okra to put over his rice. There's a real trick to cooking okra properly. A lot of people groan inside when you mention okra because they think of it as being very slimy and slippery. It is, too, unless you fix it properly. I first tasted the okra that Henry made when I was about thirteen years old and I didn't try to repeat the process myself until 1963. If this isn't it, darn it, this is almost it.

Cut the okra first and steam it in a little water for about 15 minutes to get all the slime off. Then pour the water away. Now put some oil in. Henry actually used bacon fat, and you will like it better if you stay with Henry's way. Simmer the okra in this grease, add garlic, canned tomatoes, and onions, and continue to simmer for about 20 minutes until everything is nice and done. Salt and pepper to taste. Cover the pan with the okra in it until you are ready to eat. Now steam some of that good rice like Henry did and you are in business.

HOG BRAINS

Maybe you are beginning to think that I am not going to leave much of that hog. You are right. Before this book is over, we will get around to the ham and the loin and the tail and even the feet.

You may have to acquire a taste for hog brains. I don't know, but I really like brains. You have to soak the hog's brain in warm water and salt for a while and then take a small paring knife and cut the bloody veins out. You'll find them in-between these sections. They have a name but my medical knowledge of hog or man doesn't quite go that far.

Those little sections of the cranium, wash them well. Now fry some bacon or fatback and let your purse be your guide about which one you use. You shouldn't believe those recipes that say that you have to use just a certain thing or else your cooking will be blah; most of the time you can enjoy a little flexibility there.

After cleaning the brains, put them in the grease that is left from the bacon or fatback and simmer for about 10 or 15 minutes with the pan covered. Up to this point, better not let the family watch the first time, or you'll get turned-up noses. Later, when they ask for the same dish again, hit them with it. Now beat at least 6 or 8 eggs, about 1 or 2 for each person you intend to serve. I would use 6 eggs for a couple of boxes of brains. It is hard to describe how the brains would be in pounds because they come in little containers. For my family, I get 2 and sometimes 3 boxes of brains. Add the eggs to the brains in the pan. Cook them as if you were scrambling eggs until they are done to the consistency you enjoy most. Salt and pepper. If you haven't had hog brains before, you are in for a wonderful surprise. Don't be frightened, now, hog brains are served in some of the grandest homes to the grandest folks.

PIG'S FEET
AND PIG'S TAILS

You can cook them together or cook one and not the other, because they are prepared in pretty much the same way. Now note that we are not talking about *pickled* pig's feet, but just plain old pig's feet from the butcher. I get my butcher to chop between the toes of the pig's feet. When I get them home, I singe that hair off, because pigs do have hair on their feet. Then I put them down into lots of water so that I could cook them a long time. Most people don't cook them long enough. When that water gets down very low, I add salt and pepper and sometimes a little red pepper or Tabasco. If you don't like hot pepper, and, frankly, I am not too particular about it myself, then just leave it out, that's up to you. But this is important—do add a little bit of vinegar. What do I mean by a little bit? I don't know, do what looks right and if it doesn't come out the way you want it, do it differently the next time. If you want, you can add a bit of vinegar as you eat, too.

Now with the seasonings and the vinegar in there, let the pot simmer for ½ hour longer—keep watching it, though, because it will boil down to nothing. You want to cook those pig's feet until the meat falls off the bone practically. When I serve pig's feet, you can take a fork and just push the meat away from the bone. Supply plenty of paper napkins, because your fingers are going to get pretty sticky. The fork will only suffice for so long.

Everything that I have said about cooking pig's feet is also true of pig's tails. We have a lot of fun in our house and with our friends talking about pig's feet and pig's tails, because these foods are associated with the Southern people. Many people are so hung up on religion and races and creeds that they even carry that discussion over into cooking. Actually, pig's tails must be Louis's second or third favorite dish. Geography doesn't matter too much when food is really good. He can clean that little rascal so that the white skeleton looks like it belongs in the Museum of Natural History.

HOMINY

Now I am going to tell you how to fix hominy. Not "harmony," that's my other line of work. Take careful note that hominy is not exactly the same as hominy *grits*. Plain hominy is large like marbles and hominy grits is fine and powered à la cream of farina and the likes of that.

Mama used to fry some fatback, then put the hominy in the frying pan with the grease for about

5 minutes. Add 2 cups of water, a pinch of sugar, and salt and pepper and let the mixture simmer until done. Hominy is thought to be a rather common food, and yet, properly prepared, it really is a delicacy. I particularly enjoy hominy at breakfast time.

Talking about hominy and grits makes me think of a wonderful occasion when Madame Ambassador Perle Mesta gave a supper for me in Washington. Of all things, she had a great big silver chafing dish of hominy grits. I smiled to myself because I was looking at all the socialites and ambassadors and senators as they went crazy over those grits. I was thinking how ironic it was that some people who were far away from this social level might frown greatly at having hominy grits for a social supper.

I think there must have been something about Mama's cooking that was very wholesome and good for you. I have said that it was plain food, deliciously prepared, and maybe the key was that we had our food regularly and we enjoyed eating plenty of it because Mama prepared it so well. The subject of health makes me think of something I had long forgotten about Papa. Papa ate two or three yeast cakes every day of his life. I don't know where he got the idea, or when he started it, but he seemed to know that it was good for him. I am talking about those plain old yeast cakes that you could buy at the grocery store for baking bread, at two or three cents apiece in those days. Papa ate them just the way they came out of the wrapper. I don't know whether it means anything or not, but my Papa never had a sick day until he was seventy-nine years old, and he worked hard all of his adult life.

MAMA'S CAKE

I am sure you can tell that I look back on my Mama and Papa, both now gone, with a great deal of affection. Even today I have a picture of Mama in my kitchen, looking over my shoulder, just as she did when I was eight years old. Sometimes, particularly in the night, when my thoughts and feelings run strong, I talk to that woman the same as if she were here. At those times, my memories of her, my recollection of things that happened during my childhood, come clear and vivid. On one such occasion, late at night, I sat down at my kitchen table and wrote this poem about Mama's cake.

Mama's Cake

My kitchen seems friendly today,
Warm.
Perfumed with vanilla.
Mama is making a treat—
Her cake.
It's simple,
Not a fancy one like the lady down
The street—
Who gave me a piece of hers
Yesterday.
But her kitchen didn't seem to
Smell as sweet—
Nor did I have the pleasure
Of watching her make it.

I'm watching Mama.
I smell our sweet kitchen.
Mama is here—
I'm near Mama,
And guess what—
Not only will I get some of the
Finished product,
She'll let me run my small
Fingers
Around the bowl—
To get the leavings,
What didn't get in the pan.

I like the kitchen.
I like Mama's cake.

I honestly wish that I could make Mama's cake and could tell you how it is done. It was a kind of mystical process. We didn't eat much sweet food in our house and so it wasn't very often that Mama decided to make a cake. But then on the spur of the moment Mama would get up from the table and begin to throw things into a bowl—2 to 4 cups sifted flour, 2 or 4 eggs, baking powder (about 1 teaspoon I think), vanilla flavoring and enough water to make it loose. Yes, I said water. We didn't drink a lot of milk in our house—it wasn't because we were poor, it is just that we didn't prefer it. Even on our cereal, we often had evaporated milk, or does that go back too far for you? After putting this mixture together, she would toss it into a medium oven and somehow it turned into cake. (Now came the good part—we got to lick the bowl. We ran our fingers around the side until there was absolutely nothing left, and, believe me, it tasted good.) Mama would peek into the oven occasionally and when it looked brown on top, she would pull out the tins—she cooked this in 4 or 5 little round pie tins. On the top of each one she would spread jelly or jam, whatever she happened to have, and slap them on top of each other like big pancakes. Whoosh! A four-layer cake. A lot of people think that a cake has to be fancy and have icing and all of that—not so with Mama. I can't think of any cake that I would rather have at this moment.

Mama died a few years back. I saw it coming, even before she got seriously ill. Actually, in order to clear my feelings, I wrote a kind of tribute, you might call it, an obituary, about my Mama before she died:

"I saw Mama today sitting at the kitchen table sort of there and yet not there. Virgie, my oldest sister, called this afternoon and said 'Dick [my nickname], I want to ask you a question. What do you think about Mama?' Virgie suspected something too. I think Mama sees something coming [I saw Papa at the end. I saw in his eyes a look that

I have seen in my own, at the point of death with
my heart. Now I know that it was that same look
that I saw in Mama's eyes]. Mama's eyes see the
beginning of the end. The look of it frightens me a
bit.

"This is the Mama I know, looking over all four
of us through the years. Each of us knows her in his
or her own way. To me, she has been like a lioness
watching over her cubs, teaching them all and
sending them into the world hoping they would
return to the lair from time to time. Yet, even if
they never did return, Mama felt that she had
prepared them for it. I had a moment of truth recently with Mama when we had a talk about love
and its meaning. Mama cried after that conversation. Do you know that may have been the only
time I ever saw that woman cry? We were alone
and I knew she was Love.

"In her eyes today, I saw the realization that she
cannot survive much longer. She sees herself getting older and she sees us growing farther away
from her loving hands of diaper days. You see,
Mama never quite turned loose of life's terrific
moments. Now the lioness has begun to draw away
from us all. She busies herself as much as possible
with her house and her goldfish. We never had a
house without goldfish. Mama used to talk to those
fish, and I am sure she does so more now that we
are not at home.

"She looks into the distance, all too near, and
saves her strength against the time when she will
call all of her cubs to her side to say good-bye."

Sanctuary

Y KITCHEN is a mystical place, a kind of temple for me. It is a place where the surfaces seem to have significance, where the sounds and odors carry meaning that transfers from the past and bridges to the future. It is that place in my life where the memories of Mama and Papa and my brother and sisters are located. It is a place where show business and bright lights fade away, leaving my consciousness clear for understanding. It is a room in which to find sanctuary in the enjoyment of the best lingering recollections of times gone by, a room where the circumstances of the present and the good or bad possibilities for the future can be dealt with. I don't like to say that my kitchen is actually a *religious* place, but I would say that if I were a voodoo priestess, I would conduct my rituals there.

My primary ritual in the kitchen is an exercise of sharing. It is a place where I cook for my family, whose images pervade my thoughts while I work. I cook not only for my family and loved ones, but also for unseen guests, strangers who might happen upon my door. I cook for four, but while I am in the kitchen I have the unmistakable feeling that my family is huge, including all those people of the world who might by chance receive pleasure from what I concoct. Surely for me cooking is a grand form of giving—Mama always said you never know who is going to knock at the door and be hungry. I cook for many people. It isn't that it is necessarily economical to do so, it is just that I would rather do without something fancy and cook a full pot.

My kitchen is a simple room, and I love it for that too. To my way of thinking, a kitchen must be a clean and functional place to work and a satisfactory place in which to meditate. I put things that I enjoy in there—I have a couple of clowns, cheap paintings, but pleasant to me. Also, there is the ever-present picture of Mama looking over what I do. Here and there I will pick up a dollar poster and frame it for the wall. I have a calendar with a poem on it, and a needlepoint of the Ten Commandments hangs on the kitchen door. I tell my children that that is the only religion that we have, and that if they could follow eight out of ten of them, they will be doing pretty well.

The family work chart hangs on the kitchen wall. In the corner is my portable radio and a little portable TV for news once in a while. By the way, I never turn on that television for daytime serials. I think that we have enough to deal with in the real world without going through fictitious problems all the time. I don't care who is king for the day or who is queen for the day, or whether Portia faces life or not.

In fact, I don't like to have anything in my kitchen that interferes with the main business of the room. I have a phone in there, but sometimes I actually take it off the hook in order to keep it from interfering. Someone will call me up while I am in the kitchen and just say, "How are you feeling?" And I say, "Who is it, Honey?" We talk a bit and then I say, "Well, could you call me back, because I have something on the stove." Right away then I hang up that phone—I don't like to burn my food and I really don't like to have my thoughts interrupted.

Sometimes I'll let the phone ring once and then again and finally it stops. Then, if it rings again a few minutes later, I'll pick it up because I figure then it is important. I have found out that most people have absolutely nothing to say. I simply don't like to have people call me up at nine o'clock in the morning and say, "What do you know?" The first thing that runs through my mind is, "I know a *lot*, but I am not going to tell you about it at nine o'clock in the morning. I have an office and it opens at ten."

We even have a certain technique about the phone in my office. My secretary, Dodi, always lets the phone ring at least twice. That's a good rule to use at home too. If you are a single girl and you pick it up on the first ring, your boyfriend will think that you are sitting there waiting for him to call. If you are married, and it is your husband on the phone, he'll think you aren't doing a damn thing except sitting there lazing away and waiting to grab the phone. In the office it is important never to let anyone know you are that anxious to get a message. I have also told Dodi that we do not make any calls out of our office until at least ten thirty in the morning. The reason is that I figure most businessmen don't get into their offices until ten o'clock (that used to be nine, but things have changed). Half the time when an executive gets into his office at ten o'clock he is going to take care of at least one or two of the three S's before he gets down to business, and I don't think I have to explain that to you. They concern the bathroom, a shower, and a shave. Another thing, when a man first arrives in his office, he may have left angry at the old lady, or he may have been pissed off at traffic on the way to work. Maybe the children got him upset before he left home—you know men. So let the old boy get to his office and settle himself down, and at ten thirty you will probably be able to get a darn good answer for whatever your question is. You will also find that you don't get very good answers to any kind of questions on Monday or Friday. On Mondays they are just coming back from the weekend and they haven't gotten it all together yet. Friday, they are in a hurry to get out to the weekend's activities. I start business on Tuesday. Tuesday is a very good day.

I sit in my kitchen and read a lot. I have tried to read a book a day or an article a day since I was eleven years old. And still I keep one eye on that pot over at the stove. I can catch up on a million things while fiddling in that main room. Correspondence is an example. Some of my best letters to intimate friends have been written right there at the kitchen table. I remember one time the thought seized me to answer a letter long overdue. I didn't even leave the kitchen, I just grabbed the scissors and cut the back of a grocery bag and sort of for laughs I wrote my letter right on that bag. I enjoy the spontaneity that is possible in the kitchen. Maybe that is one reason why I am not too careful about the precise quantities that go into recipes. Once in a while I will swear to myself that I am going to follow a recipe exactly and I can't seem to do it. It isn't as much fun that way. Frankly, I admire those of you who manage to go on your own once in a while. Even if you goof up on something now and then, the kitchen is a place for self-expression and you have to inject a bit of yourself into what you are doing. A director can tell a player how the role is to be played, and yet I think a good director is always looking for the player to feel something and to include himself to the point of tasting the part and seasoning it. The great director is one who whets your appetite so that you begin to believe what you are doing.

The kitchen is not a place for pretending, however. If you cook the greatest gourmet dish in the world and it turns out the way it is supposed to, you may not even be able to pronounce the name of it because it is so French. You may not even be able to describe it or to understand the significance that the dish has for the people who invented it. I have pondered that and I really believe that you cannot fully enjoy a dish under those circumstances. There is no place for pretense in my kitchen—I believe in simplicity, cleanliness, nutrition, and good flavor. I believe in cooking those things that have meaning for me and things that I understand. All of this adds to the honesty and comforting atmosphere of my kitchen.

When I taste something on the stove, I am thinking about how it is going to affect the people who will have it on the table later. I eat to live and not the reverse, so if it seems to you that I must eat a lot because I talk about food so much and with such pleasure, I just want you to know it is not the case. The preparation is my pleasure and watching others eat fills me.

As you can well imagine, it just kills me to burn food. I have said that I don't like to have intrusions into the kitchen while I am busy, and that is because it distresses me so much to ruin something. Now I am going to have to confess that I am a bread burner—I am a *regular* bread burner. Actually, we don't eat a lot of bread in our house, but we do like to have toast in the morning. From Christmases through the years and from gifts in-between, I always seem to have five or six toasters of the highest quality. I don't use any of them. I still put butter on the bread and put it in the oven under the broiler. It is the old-fashioned way and that's how I am. I turn on the broiler, put the bread in there, and burn it. I don't know why I can't remember to take it out on time. I also don't really understand why I won't pull out one of those toasters from under the cabinet and plug it in. I guess I still have in the back of my mind the memories of people who did such a beautiful job of toasting bread on top of an old black wood stove. They would take out the bread, slice it, and lay it right on top with a fork. Then they would turn it over once and it was divine. If they got a little burned corner on it, they would do what I do— scrape that right off and eat it like it was the best bread they had ever had.

I talk to myself and to the walls and to my food in the kitchen. I'll say, "Now let's see, Louis likes this so much, boy, is he going to love it when he finds out that I've cooked this today," or I'll say, "This is Tony's favorite, and Dee Dee hasn't had this since last summer."

While I am doing all of this talking, I include my dogs in it. We have three very big dogs, the kind with long fangs, teeth that could tear up a tiger. I don't think it is fair for these poor dogs to be stuck with canned food that you can munch with no teeth at all. That stuff reminds me of mush, like people had many years ago. If I am cooking some special hamburger, I find I'll just pinch off a little piece here and there for the dogs, especially if I have had three good strong show-business jobs in a row and feel a little rich. After I have pinched off three pinches, I step to the back door and have a little conversation with the dogs. I make them sit down and eat like ladies and gentlemen. Of course, that little bite of hamburger goes down pretty fast, but we have a few minutes to sit there together while they are licking their mouths. Did you ever notice how a dog will lick and lick after he has had something good to eat, even if it was only a tiny morsel?

With the dogs in mind I once said to the butcher, "Could I please have a couple of the big soup bones?" He went into the back and came up with a couple of bones that looked like they must have been from an elephant. He said, "Pearl, if you want some more, I have plenty." I said, "Great," and he filled me a whole bag. Now of course I gave the dogs just one bone each. The rest I put in the freezer. After that I pulled one out about six weeks later for each dog. I know it takes that long to bury a bone and dig it up six or seven times until they are through with it.

In show business, I always have closed rehearsals —music rehearsals—when I am going to do a show on TV or the stage. I allow no one in there but the people involved. The audience is there in my mind. That's what is important; the same thing applies to my cooking. I am always hoping for that favorable audience in the club or theater or at the dinner table. I cook the way I entertain. The key is that what I am doing has to come deep from my insides, with great feeling.

I draw only a very fine line between physical nourishment and emotional nourishment. When I was a little girl, I sat in our parlor only on Sundays when I had my best dress on. Even then I found that not a particularly exciting place to be. Why should I be in there when I could be hanging close to the kitchen with things happening? Throughout my young life and right up to the present, I have received both kinds of nourishment from that room in our house. It is the one place where the physical and the emotional come together for me.

This business about the two kinds of nourishment may explain why I have put such importance on the U.S.O. I have taken a number of tours for that organization, and I think it is very important. They say that the army travels on its stomach. Well, I think that is part of the truth. The fact is that people, wherever they are, need all kinds of nourishment, comfort, and support. My feeling for the U.S.O. is not a political deal—it has nothing to do with whether I am pro or con war. To me the U.S.O. means that I can do something for our boys who are away from home. None of them really wants to live under the circumstances of war; they all want to be home and they all need to see a friend. They need to hear about familiar places. When you walk into a U.S.O. club overseas, everybody becomes your brother or your cousin. They don't want to talk about war, they just want to say I'm from New Jersey or I'm from Connecticut or Georgia. That means something to them—it is nourishing. What are all of these thoughts doing in a cookbook? I guess that they just occur to me naturally as I sit at my kitchen table thinking about the pleasure of giving.

Indeed, the kitchen is a place for considerations of giving. It is a place where most of the time those to whom you would give are close in your mind.

Once in a while, I find that loneliness overtakes me in the kitchen. Sharing and meditation and thanksgiving give way to feelings of isolation. Once this summer such feelings came to me as I thought of someone special. I wrote this poem:

Alone in My Kitchen

Thoughts of you come fast and beautiful.
It is lonely here in my kitchen without you.
You would like the warmth of my kitchen today,
Though I would have to smack your fingers
If you would lift my pot tops,
Which irks me;
Or dig into that pot with a spoon,
Not being able to wait.
Why would you even be there?
You know the rule is "No company in the kitchen."
I know why—
Because your possesiveness makes you feel
You own every other room,
So you decide to sit in the kitchen and wait,
And for that
I love you.

JEAN'S BEANS
(Jean DiMaio)

It was in Boston that beans really came into prominence. Someone took a bean, mixed in a few ingredients, baked it, and Boston Baked Beans were born. I find that every cookbook, or at least two-thirds of them, has a recipe for baked beans. Of course now baked beans are served in every state and in many foreign countries. But "Boston" is still in front of the word "beans."

Now hear this. I have a friend, a good friend, who is from Colorado. She is half Osage Indian and doesn't know a bean about Boston. But she bakes the best pot of beans in the world. One day, knowing her generous heart, I called Jean DiMaio and asked for her recipe. She gave it freely.

I wouldn't say that my beans turned out like Jean's, but they were delicious. The kind of delicious that should be spelled *d-e-e-l-i-s-h-u-s*. Like mine, your beans might not taste exactly like Jean's, but then you would never know that because you have never tasted hers. As a matter of fact, the secret ingredient is the warmth of Jean. Everyone doesn't have that; everyone doesn't have so much love to put into the beans as she makes them. If you could just get close, be thankful for that, as I am.

Start with 2 large cans of pork and beans, baked beans, or your own cooked navy beans. If you use your own cooked beans, you will have to double all the seasoning in this recipe. Place in a large oiled casserole the following ingredients: the beans, 1 chopped onion (medium or large), 2 tablespoons of mustard (prepared), ¼ cup of dark molasses, 2 heaping tablespoons of brown sugar, ½ to ¾ cup of ketchup (hot is better), at least 1 cup of shredded sharp cheese (the more the merrier). Mix all ingredients well, sprinkle the top with more cheese and bake 45 to 60 minutes at 350°. Let the pot stand at least 15 or 20 minutes before serving. Incredible!

JEAN'S BROCCOLI
(Jean DiMaio)

Broccoli was never really part of my bit until I tasted the broccoli that Jean made. Here's how she does it: Separate the stems so that you have medium-size pieces, wash thoroughly and sprinkle with salt, pepper, and garlic powder. Set it aside. Heat some oil in a fairly deep and wide pan. Chop a little garlic into the oil and brown it, then remove the garlic pieces. Add the broccoli to the pan, but be careful because the water on the broccoli may pop when you place it in hot oil. Once it is in the pan, sprinkle a little more water on the broccoli, cover the pan and let it steam until the broccoli is tender, turning when necessary. This is especially good if you allow the broccoli to brown in the oil, but you must watch it very closely or it will burn. Broccoli like this finds its way to my table fairly often now. Thanks to Jean, broccoli has become a delicacy to my family.

It is a turning world—the kitchen is the place where life, death, love, and hate all walk in and are rewarded or healed. When babies are born, the first thing they do after they have their fannies patted to start that precious breath going, is to reach for nourishment—food from the mother's breast. Before you know it, the rascal is sitting at the table screaming his or her head off for real honest-to-goodness food. By now, he feels that milk is okay, but he is looking for meat. As the child grows, he has his best conversations with his mother in that kitchen where things are safe and warm and comfortable. When the child leaves home, it is in the kitchen that the mother thinks of him most often. When death removes a loved one, I find that those left behind tend to congregate in the kitchen. If there is to be weeping and gnashing of teeth, wailing and beating of walls during the time of terrible hurt, it is best in the kitchen. I have had loving friends and family come into my kitchen to be nourished in time of mutual loss. I cook and we all try to make laughter while tears come. We speak of the dead in great and glowing terms, and finally get down to messages of assurance and love. The coffee is heated and reheated. Finally they eat.

Then, as I have seen it happen, the hurt can come out in anger—brothers and friends become enemies for a moment. Feelings run high as death sits down and has a hot cup of coffee while we humans mull cold cups. Then as if because he is in the kitchen, someone recovers all at once and realizes the closeness that is there. The dead in a sense return from the grave at that moment. Death's coffee gets cold and ours recovers its warmth. We come to our senses and realize that the kitchen can hold us all, united in love.

That is the kind of room it is—my best memories

of those who are now in the great spiritual world come from times when I have talked with them in their kitchens or mine, and now somehow I know that they live on in my own kitchen as they live no place else. My kitchen can hold us all.

Simple Satisfaction

N A CERTAIN respect, I think the cave men had something going for them back in those times. After all, stop and think about it—they had very simple foods which they cooked over a fire in that one big pot. I'm not what you might call a Stone Age lady (except that I do like a diamond here and there), but I do like simplicity in the kitchen and at the dinner table. I enjoy one-pot cooking, and I am not fond of long complicated recipes that call for ingredients that nobody ever heard of.

Don't get me wrong. I do enjoy those wonderful sauces that the French serve. When I was there I thought that the atmosphere in the restaurant was wonderful and some of that food really was a delight to have as a special treat. My point is that people don't have to eat elaborate food to eat well, and they do not have to have multiple-course dinners to feel that they have done an adequate job with dinner. There are people in this country, even poor people some of whom are on relief, who feel that they have to have a six-course dinner or they are not eating. That is a definite lie. The one-pot meal is still better from every point of view as far as I am concerned. You can enjoy the meal just as much and you can save some money, not to mention the time involved in preparing the meal. One of my purposes in this book is to recommend economy and simplicity in choosing and preparing food. I detest going to the market and spending sixty-nine cents for one green pepper just because some recipe calls for green pepper. That gets a bit too far away from reality for me.

I think many people prefer to think that many celebrities eat sparrow tongues for breakfast, lunch, and dinner, or maybe even sparrow tongues with green peppers added. The assumption seems to be that if a celebrity likes it, it must be good, or if the President of the U.S. does it, it must be right, or if the millionaire has it, it must be the thing to strive for. There were ninety-six people at the White House when I had dinner there most recently. I did enjoy it, but to tell you the truth I think that they might have done just as well with some of my lima beans and macaroni and cheese. After dinner, maybe there wouldn't have been so many long speeches, everybody would have been just too happy and satisfied and sleepy to sit there in those straight chairs.

There are about five million cookbooks on the market and it takes almost five million dollars to cook the average recipe in any one of them. Some of those recipes are not worth the time and money that's required to prepare them. I hold to simple cooking no matter who is coming to my house as a guest. First I should say that we don't have very many guests at our house. But occasionally we have someone who is generally considered to be an important person. When I start to plan a meal like that I always say to myself, "Well now, they are just people and there is something that everyone can appreciate." Everyone who eats in my house is important to me. It just does not make any sense to change your cooking because someone is coming over. If the husband is bringing an executive home with him, it makes no sense for the wife to spend three days ahead of time preparing and planning that meal. The simple fact is that Mr. So-and-So would probably faint with joy if he could get a piece of corn bread. The simple things have a way of winning people over, making them comfortable, and impressing them in a way that no fancy food could equal. The millionaire and the bum on the street have the same stomach.

People who want to make the big impression sometimes do it with cooking, but other times they will try to show how much they can prepare or how fancy they can make the table look. My table is as simple as my cooking, no matter who sits down. I do like a tablecloth. In the early days of my show-business career, I ate on too many oilcloth table-cloths and dirty wooden tabletops. I set a clean table, but not necessarily with a bowl of flowers and the fancy china and the special stemware and the heavy silver.

I've got the china all right. It is still in the china closet with the silver cups that you might use for wine. One day years ago, I ran across an auction gallery down in Florida. I looked in the window and saw a salt and pepper shaker that I wanted. While I was in there, I happened to spy a beautiful platter. I like great big platters because I put several kinds of meats on the same one, and the really big ones are hard to find. Well, I got the platter and while I was picking it up I happened to see a glass and then my eye moved and I saw a whole set of this stuff, dipped in gold or whatever it was, and that started a chain of events. I ended up buying $500 worth of stuff. The funny thing is that as much as I like these beautiful things, they have never been on my table. Oh, I mean they were *fancy,* laid in with all kinds of intricate work. They are just gorgeous and they have never been touched. You might be interested to know what I do put on the table. I am still eating on some crockery that I bought twenty years ago. One day in Las Vegas I was walking down Fremont Street and I stopped to look into a store that belonged to Rex Bell, who used to be married to Clara Bow. It was sort of a Western store. I saw some dishes with steer heads all painted around, a sort of ranch crockery. I loved those dishes. I didn't buy the set then, but I thought about it over and over again. Then in 1953 I was walking down Fifth Avenue and I saw that same set of dishes in W. & J. Sloane's and bought it. To this day, only three pieces have been broken. The kids managed to take care of the three pieces with their special dish washing. Last Christmas my niece gave me a set of dishes and I put them away too.

Speaking of simplicity at the table, here is one of the good and simple things I serve on my simple plates.

HAMBURGER CASSEROLE PEARL

Mix salt and pepper into the hamburger thoroughly (I seldom start with less than 6 pounds of meat), then spread a layer of hamburger all across the bottom of a roasting pan. Sprinkle with chopped parsley, onion, and cheese. Over the top of this, sprinkle enough rice so that you can't see the hamburger any more—about ⅛ inch of cooked rice. Then put on another layer of hamburger, more parsley, onion, and cheese, and a bit more rice. Keep repeating this process until you run out of hamburger. If you like to use Accent, as I do, it will make this dish even better. By the way, I hope that the consumers' bureaus or the medical people don't find something wrong with Accent. It seems to me they always find that something is unhealthy about the time I begin to dig it.

After you have cooked this roasting-pan casserole about ¾ done (it takes about 1 hour in a 350° oven) pour 1 can of tomatoes over it—not tomato paste or sauce, but the real tomatoes. Let it simmer for about 15 minutes with the top on.

BAKED BEEF WITH CHEESE

This is a variation on the hamburger casserole, for times when you need fewer servings and you don't want leftovers. Just listen to the ingredients and see if your wig doesn't flip right off: 1 pound of ground beef, 1 cup of rice, 1 onion, 2 tablespoons of oil, salt, pepper, paprika, and a few olives, stuffed or not. Two cups of tomato juice and 1½ cups of grated cheese. Are you still with me?

Cook the ground beef, rice, and chopped onion in a little oil until lightly brown. Pour off the drippings. Season with salt, pepper, and paprika, add olives, enough tomato juice to make the mixture soupy, and a bit of water. Place all of this in a casserole, cover tightly, and cook for 1 hour at 350°. Then uncover and sprinkle with grated cheese. Continue baking for 10 minutes or until the cheese melts through. This will serve 6 people.

POLISH SAUSAGE AND POTATOES

I keep the radio on in my kitchen and it seems to me that every few days they announce another price rise. The economical recipes may be more important than any of us thought. Mama used to fix a dish that was simple, but delicious and filling. She boiled potatoes and Polish sausage in the same pot. Those sausages make the potatoes taste wonderful. You don't have to be poor to love this dish.

I often wonder what would happen if we would go on a simplicity strike for a while in this country. Maybe we could bring some of those big food companies to their senses, or shall we forever wait on Ralph Nader to save the world (or whatever he is trying to do).

In case you don't know what Polish sausages are, they are the long brown ones and your butcher can help you. Four or 5 sausages will feed my family of four. You just put the sausage in water, boil it (uncovered), cut your potatoes in squares or quarters and throw them right in on top. Boil this mixture down and then take maybe a couple of teaspoons of flour and enough water in a cup to make a smooth paste. Add that to the pot with salt and pepper, and that's all there is to it. Simmer down. It is deceptively easy, but your family will want this dish over and over again.

KNOCKWURST AND BEANS

This is not really a recipe, but just a recommended combination of good things—the Polish sausage up above made me think of it. I get the nice big fat knockwurst and steam it in a small amount of water—they pop open quickly that way. Then I dress up some canned pork and beans—what the heck, they are only canned beans and they need a little help sometimes. I put in a little salt and pepper and add about ¼ pound of butter to 2 very large cans of beans. Then I add about 3 tablespoons and even a dash more of sugar. Finally, I boil them long enough so that they get thicky. (Well, if I make up my own dishes, then I ought to be able to make up some of my own words.) We have a good green salad and that makes our meal. That, by the way, is a favorite dinnertime meal for my children.

PLAIN OLD VEGETABLE SOUP

How many days I have gone to the store, even when I had a job and a little money in my pocket, and asked the butcher for a big bag of plain soup bones. There's no meat on these bones, but the marrow is good for soup. When I get those bones home, I am already thinking of how good that soup is going to be. While I am boiling the bones, I get me 4 or 5 packs of good frozen vegetables and drop them in the pot as soon as the bones have boiled enough to get the marrow and the juice out. Now if fresh vegetables are in season and are particularly good, I use them instead of frozen vegetables. But to tell you the truth, it doesn't make a great deal of difference in soup. The frozen ones are best if you're in a hurry. Once I have those vegetables and the bones boiling away, I throw in a few onions and some parsley and whatever else delectable I may lay my hands on. And very often I will put some noodles in there too. While that is simmering away, I make a pan of corn bread and, Honey, that's what we have for dinner and there is nothing wrong with it. When it's all over, I take the bones out of there and the dogs love them. Usually, I have enough soup to put some away in the freezer.

CHICKEN SOUP

Where did the expression "Jewish penicillin" come from? Referring to chicken soup this way really implies no disrespect, I guess, for the Jewish people, because surely they must make the best chicken soup of all. Some say that it has real curative powers, but all I know is that it is very, very good to eat. I get a good kosher chicken when I can, because kosher chickens are so very fresh. I put the chicken in the pot, fill it about ½ full with water (or however much soup I intend to make), add salt, pepper, and if I have some onions, I throw them in too. I put the pan, covered, over a high flame until it starts to boil, and then I turn it down halfway and cook very slowly. Generally, I let my soup simmer down so that the water point is fairly low and the soup is concentrated. Label it whatever you want, it's a wonderful soup. I enjoy it particularly in the wintertime. Throw in some vegetables. That's the *pièce de résistance*. That's French.

BEANS—LIMA BEANS, NAVY BEANS, BLACK-EYED PEAS

All of them are cooked the same way. The same recipe covers a multitude of beans. Sometimes when I have cooked a big pot of beans, I will serve them day after day. Beans keep well in the refrigerator, but you should make sure when you rewarm them that you use a very low fire. Nothing can burn as fast as beans. If you turn your head for a second, they will stick to the bottom of the pot and that's it.

Some people soak their beans overnight in cold water, saying it makes them tender and cook quicker. I don't bother. I just wash them in cold water, clean them very well. As I pour them out of the bag, I always look for those little pieces of black grit. I fill the pot about ¾ full of water. Add bacon, ham, bacon grease, or fatback. Then start the flame on high and turn it down after the pot comes to a boil. Add beans. Cover, cook slowly until they are done—about 1½ hours. When the water begins to ride low in the pan, and looks milky white, I know that the beans are just beautiful. Then, of course, I season with salt and pepper.

I love to cook ham and save the juice. Have you ever tried it? I put it right into milk bottles or other containers and keep it in the refrigerator for all my vegetable cooking. You really don't need a piece of meat every time you want to season vegetables or cook more beans. It doesn't make sense. Whenever I boil a ham, I add plenty of water so that I'll have quite a bit of juice left over after cooking. This doesn't work too well with precooked ham, so I get them raw.

Here's another little trick that you ought to know about beans. If you keep dried beans for a long time before cooking them they can get fairly tough. My Mama used to toss in a pinch of baking soda for a pot of beans. It acts as a tenderizer. Baking soda will also tenderize meat or any vegetable if the leaves are tough. I quite often have beans for a good while before I get around to cooking them all because I buy them up in advance. When I have had two or three good jobs in a row, I go to the store and stock up on things like beans. I also get doubles and triples of things like soap and I'll buy twelve or fifteen rolls of toilet paper and paper towels and put them away. I guess I have Mama's expression ringing in my ears telling me that you never know when you are not going to be working.

If you really want to have beans the way I learned to eat them when I was growing up, you have to get ham hocks or neck bones to throw in there with the beans. Neck bones in particular lend a special flavor to a pot of beans that can't be duplicated in any other way.

HAMBURGER
ALL THE WAY

I get these ready in advance and wrap them in foil and put them in the icebox. That way I am ready at dinnertime for a late snack. I do 6 or 8 or 10 pounds of hamburger at once, because my family can knock these off pretty fast, especially in the summer when I have loads of children around visiting my pool. In a mixing bowl I combine hamburger, chopped onion, salt, pepper, and load the mixture with eggs. I shape them into balls and wrap them in foil. When the occasion arises, I take them out of the icebox and bake them at 300°. They are better baked than broiled—nice and juicy. I sometimes cook them on the barbecue out by the pool.

I really don't like to hear people talk about what they call "Soul Food." In fact, I don't really appreciate having any group of foods associated with certain minorities or nationalities. Too often, that kind of talk is used to sort of make fun of certain groups of people. It might even serve to keep folks from trying some pretty good food sometimes, just because they think it is not for them. Good food, really good food, well prepared, is dignified and worthwhile for anyone no matter what his race or his nationality or station in life.

Certainly different people and different parts of the country have come up with unique dishes, but any kind of people from any part of the world will eat practically any food if they get a taste of it properly prepared. Sometimes they use eating habits to show that they are better than other people. I am here to tell you one thing for sure—food in India can be wonderful, or in Italy, or Poland, or England, or Mississippi, or New York City. If you look for the honest beauty in people and food, and if you eat to please yourself and no one else, then *all food is food of the soul.*

HARD-SHELL CRABS IN BEER

When I was little, we used to go down to the wharf in Washington, D.C., down by the Potomac River, and buy hard-shell crabs by the bushel. In Washington and Baltimore they really made the hard-shell crabs. They've changed all that now, and I don't suppose you can buy them so easily or so inexpensively any more. I know that the old wharf is gone now, the way of the crab boats. There is a freeway or something crossing the place where it used to be. We would get 6 or 7 dozen hard-shell crabs. I remember they were really something else when they got to crawling around. Just getting them in the pot was a big deal.

Most people cook crabs in water, but that isn't the best way. After all, they've just come out of the water. Instead of that, get 2 or 3 cans of beer and pour it in a big pot. Add some red-hot peppers or some Tabasco, a bit of salt and pepper, and toss in those crabs. Put them in only when it's boiling hot, so they get the message quickly. *And this is important*—put something heavy on the top of that pot to hold them down. It doesn't matter how many of them you put in there, but get them steaming hot. Of course, if you have really a lot of crabs, you might get 6 cans of beer. Now let those babies steam. When they are done and you open one of those crabs, that juice runs everyplace and the taste is really out of this world. When they turn *red,* they are ready—about 15 to 20 minutes. Don't bother with plates. Spread out newspaper, get the paper napkins, and go.

≋≋≋≋

TURNIP GREENS, MUSTARD GREENS, DANDELIONS

≋≋≋

The same basic treatment for them all—wash the greens, and I mean really wash them thoroughly, because there is nothing worse than gritty greens. I go leaf by leaf. Go ahead and wash them in detergent, as my sister Eura does, but get them clean! I want every single tiny piece of grit off there before I start the cooking. The suds wash helps get all the sprays and everything off the vegetables. By the way, what did farmers' wives do years ago? Weren't bugs in style then?

Frozen greens are a poor compromise—they simply don't taste as good, so forget about them. You may have to grow your own greens. Now I'm not a farmer and it's really funny to watch me try to plant a flower, but when we lived on the ranch in Apple Valley, California, I just scratched that hard desert dirt to plant my greens. That earth was good and dry at 110° some days. Fortunately, you can plant turnip greens along a very shallow row. Mine were certainly shallow, because the sun was beaming down and my back was breaking. Finally, I pushed the dirt over the seeds with my foot gently, and watered my magic plot every day faithfully. Ten days later, with the watering and the sun, I let out a yelp; I saw life! A tip of green sticking out of there! They should have had that yell on TV advertising something else. Now I do the same thing every year in my backyard in the San Fernando Valley. The point is that I want us to be able to have greens every day if we want them.

I don't know what the medical world will say about this, but I want to tell you that the juice from all greens is good to drink. That juice can tune your body up and regulate it in more ways than one. It is called "pot likker." Recently, I heard of someone who canned it and was making a fortune. That old drink is as old as the hills.

Anyway, after washing the greens and rinsing them well, I put them in a pot that is about ¼ full of water. It is important to remember that greens carry their own water, too, and a great deal of it, so you don't need to add too much to the pot. Adding too much water, you could make them soggy. If you are going to season with meat, such as ham, it's as well to put that into the pot while you are still washing the greens. That gives the meat a head start when everything starts to cook. Season with salt and pepper. Put the top on there after it comes to a medium boil, and then don't fool around. Keep checking back with it, tasting to see if everything is almost done. When they are almost finished, take the top off and leave it off while the water boils down considerably. Keep in mind that you are going to concentrate that pot likker and keep it. You can pour off some of the juice and save it and then let the greens cook a little more. How good it used to be when Mama would turn around from the stove and hand each of us a cup of hot pot likker!

GREASY GREENS

Absolutely wild. Some people like smothered greens and some don't. To start with, you boil the greens only about half as long as you would for the recipe above. In other words, for sure, they don't get fully done. Then in a frying pan cook a slice of ham or some salt pork or some fatback until the grease comes out—or should I be prim and proper and say the *oil* or the *fat*. Now when I say salt pork, or fatback, I may create a problem for you. Sometimes these days you have to break your fanny driving around to different stores to find what you want, especially if you live in certain parts of the country. You see, years ago, fatback was considered poor folk's bacon, and now, if prices keep going up, it is going to be rich folk's bacon. Take the greens out of the pot and put them in the skillet. According to your own preference, you may or may not remove the pork before you do this. Chop the greens up into little pieces right there in the pan. Add water (not too much, about 1¼ cups). Cover the skillet and let it simmer. Lawdy!

A word of caution about salt pork—some of it is very salty and some of it is not very salty at all. Wait until everything is done and do a little tasting there before you add extra salt to the pot. Once your family gets a taste of this, they will help you plant your next batch of greens. You and all of your family will smack your chops on these goodies. "Chops"—that's the late Louis Armstrong's word for lips.

SPINACH WITH OIL AND GARLIC

While I am on the subject of greens, I am going to tell you about something else terrific. Cook the spinach ¾ done in barely enough water to do the job, then pour off the excess water and pour in some cooking oil (as much as you and your family like). Then add oodles and oodles of garlic cut in very tiny pieces. Add salt and pepper. Simmer. If you have been eating spinach about once a year, the old way, then please do try it this way. I think it may change your schedule to once or twice a week.

BEETS AND BEET TOPS

Beets are another thing that I cooked almost every day on the ranch. I just simply boil them in their skins. Get 6 or 8 bunches of beets (they are very reasonable), slice them, boil them (40 minutes to an hour, or until a fork will go through), and store them in a big bowl. Then you can prepare them various ways quickly. You can take a few sliced beets out and put butter on them, warm them, and eat them that way. Sometimes, I take them out and put a little vinegar and sugar on them, and they are very tasty. They are good for you too.

Many people just automatically throw away beet tops. My Mama used to cut off those beet tops and cook them. They are very tangy, and I think that it makes no sense to throw them away because, after all, they are greens. You can do anything with beet tops that you can do with any other kind of green leafy vegetable.

PORK CHOPS AND GREEN APPLES

I had a dinner a few nights ago that was more exciting, actually sexier, than a best-selling novel. What, you may ask, does sex have to do with food? Darlin', I am not going into that right now. Just let me tell you that what got me so excited was pork chops, buttered rice, and Mama's cabbage.

I always fry chops very slowly in ¼ pound (1 stick) of butter. I brown them very well, but I do not bread them. I very seldom put flour on any kind of cooking; to me meat is meat and bread is bread. Breaded chops in restaurants around the theatrical circuits broke me of the habit. The fact is in some of those places you get a lot more flour than meat.

When the chops are about ¾ done, I throw in some sliced green apples. Then I add some salt and pepper, a dash of sugar (brown is great), and sometimes a bit of nutmeg. I cover the whole thing with aluminum foil and fry it the rest of the way.

My daughter Dee Dee and my nieces, Pearlie Mae, Mary, and Candy were at the table. At one time or another all of these girls have had a problem with not being good eaters, and it really gave me a thrill to see them sit there and eat in silence. Candy ended up so full that her stomach was practically hurting. There was nothing wrong with her really except that she was just all puffed out. Pearlie Mae finally gave up and Dee Dee and Mary just kept on eating. It was a real joy for me to see them go after it that way—their little mouths sealed except for a little peephole to keep shoving that food in.

We'll take care of telling you about cabbage somewhere in this book, and I already told you how to prepare rice the way Henry did. I say that there is no gourmet food in the world that can compete with the "Plain-Ole-Down-Home-Put-Your-Feet-under-the-Table" type of dinner.

GRAVY

Years ago I had a bad scene with a friend (a man yet) who happened to intrude in my kitchen while I was making gravy. I had the meat juice all hot and ready. I got out some flour, and then I picked up a glass of water and started to add it to the flour to smooth it out. That caught his eye and he said, "Don't put that in there." This man thought of himself as a half-assed cook, too. He said he knew a little something about cooking and his mother put milk in there. I said my mother used water and her gravy was plain but good. Actually, my mother's gravy was better than most people's roast.

GRAVY PLAIN BUT GOOD

If you want to make some good gravy, do it this way. You start with the drippings in the pan. Add some butter and a little flour. Brown it in the pan slowly. Then, gradually, put just a little water in. Already you have terrific gravy as you stir it and let it simmer. Now if you really want to season it up, cut up a little bit of onion in it. Finally, I always throw in a little Accent and that tops it off. Tasty!

Talking about gravy makes me think of something that I will throw in here for free, just for newlyweds and noncooks. Do you know how to thicken? Once in a while I do find a pretty good cook who is not aware that you can add thickness to a juice in a pot of food. Boiling it down can take a long time. The trick is to take a couple of table-spoons of flour and mix it with cold water in a cup. Gradually mix it until it is smooth, then pour it into the food while it finishes cooking. You really shouldn't do this until it is done, or almost done.

I really doubt that anyone needs three full meals a day. Dinner is my main meal and I am not really fond of breakfast. Come to think about it, I guess that a lot of times there isn't much difference in timing between dinner and breakfast for me. In show business, we find ourselves keeping crazy hours sometimes when we are working. My own feeling now is that breakfast doesn't necessarily call for certain types of food and nothing else. When we were very little, Mama would sometimes warm over dinner, and we would have that for breakfast be-fore going to school. It was filling and nourishing, and we liked it very much.

The middle meal, lunch, is in a very bad condi-tion in this country now. Business people either grab some kind of cheap sandwich or a doughnut at noontime or else they have what is called a business lunch. I don't like business lunches, because I think that the two things really do not mix. Going to lunch to talk business is a mistake, although it is a very popular thing to do in many circles. One of the problems is the martini—sometimes two martinis and sometimes even three. That by itself can keep you from getting anything done at lunch. People can get so stoned that they never get to the business, and of course that calls for them to meet for lunch again the next day. If I have basic business to take care of with anyone, I would rather talk about it in an office where we can get to it.

Housewives probably do not need to eat much lunch, especially if they are in the habit of having a good breakfast. For myself, I do a very light job of it at both breakfast and lunch. Truthfully though, I do feel better if I can manage a *bit* of break-fast. Even toast or half a grapefruit or a hard-boiled egg in the morning is better than nothing and coffee.

GOOD COFFEE

A recipe for coffee? Nope, I'm just going to say a few things about coffee appreciation. I simply love a good cup of coffee once in a while, like every morning as a matter of fact.

I maintain that women have mind (and men have muscle), but at night I think the brain sort of turns way down to low. When I wake up in the morning, I think I have to do something to get that baby going again. A single cup of good coffee consumed in absolute peace is the best answer there is. Everybody in my house is in danger in the morning until I have that cup of coffee in my hand. Ah! sweet mystery—the first sip is worth all my money—it is worth all of the furs and diamonds that I might be able to get! I can look at a cup of coffee and classify it right away according to my own private little rating system. Here's how it goes:

(1) Instant coffee—any kind of instant coffee. If you make it regularly, then I say shame on you. I say that that is for an L.A. only—and I think you can figure out what L.A. stands for. It's emergency time when I resort to instant coffee.

(2) Beige coffee—this is coffee that looks and tastes like slightly dirty, warm brown water. If anything was printed at the bottom of the cup, like the maker's name, you could read it perfectly well. Very poor coffee.

(3) Medium brown coffee—not too weak and not too strong. My type. I rate this coffee excellent.

(4) Dark brown coffee—this was Mama's type of coffee, and many well-known coffee drinkers think this is the best kind. They love the strong coffee.

(5) Ink—restaurants are fond of serving this kind of coffee. Bad restaurants, and also some good ones, end up putting coffee on the table that is just like ink. Probably the pot has not been washed thoroughly for years. Then they make the coffee in the morning and let it sit there and brew all day.

Even in their homes, some people leave the pot on the stove with a small flame underneath all day long. It's really rough, that coffee, by afternoon. I say wash your coffee pot thoroughly before each new brewing of coffee.

I don't measure my coffee, I just sort of feel around and pour. Maybe 3 or more scoops to a large pot. I never overbrew coffee. I boil it, first a rapid boil, then immediately to a simmer. Then I drink it. I never use the basket inside my coffeepot. By the way, it is okay to reheat good coffee. It has been done for hundreds of years. If coffee is too dark to start with, there isn't anything you can do to make it better. Adding water to this coffee only makes weaker bad coffee. And in a restaurant I have often tried putting a little cream in the ink they serve. All that does is to turn it the most gorgeous purple you have ever seen. All you need is about four cups of that and two cigarettes and your tongue is completely finished.

The best coffee of all really isn't on my rating system. It is coffee cooked in a saucepan outdoors. I love that outdoors smell. Let's get a campaign on for some good coffee, get the restaurants to wash those pots. And at home, let's turn the fire off when the coffee is ready, and not turn it on again unless we want to reheat it later.

CORN FRITTERS

One night I had crocheted so much, I was cockeyed. So I walked around a little bit and lay back on the sofa at the hotel where I was staying and I thought of corn fritters. I thought, gee whizz, I slipped up, I don't know when I have made corn fritters. Then I remembered that Louis likes to eat raw corn; in fact, he likes corn any way at all. So I knew he would like corn fritters. Many is the time, while we've been driving along the road, my husband has pulled over to a fruit stand he has bought some apples and some corn. Some people have given

Louis the nickname "Apples" because he is 'so fond of them. Anyway, he would just shuck a piece of corn and eat it raw.

Corn fritters are divine for breakfast, dinner, or anytime. It's particularly nice in the morning if you have say a little left-over corn cooked in the refrigerator. Just mix up 1 or 2 cups of flour, 2 or 3 eggs, and about 3 cups of milk and toss in a couple of dabs of sugar and a pinch of baking powder. You mix all of that up sort of like pancake mix, and add the corn. How much corn you put in there is entirely up to you. We generally like to put a lot of it. Instead of fresh milk you can use diluted evaporated milk or even water if your pocketbook is a little tight. After you have this batter all mixed, you grab a stick of butter. Now the margarine people aren't going to like this, but in my own recipes I don't use the stuff. I jumped straight from lard to butter, and never mind that yellow stuff in-between. If you don't have the butter, you can use bacon grease. Put it maybe an ⅛ or ¼ of an inch deep in the bottom of the skillet and get it hot, but not so hot it starts to burn. Then you take a big spoon and drop that pancake in there. Just let it bubble away until it browns, then turn it over. Try some syrup over them or apple butter—yummy.

FRIED APPLES

You want to hear about something else that is really out of this world? Peel and slice some green apples into hot bacon fat. Add water. (And don't get spattered!) Sprinkle with 2 to 4 tablespoons of brown (or white) sugar. More if you like. Cover and simmer for 15 to 20 minutes. Serve with bacon and hot biscuits (store-bought or homemade).

Any kind of bread is a problem for me. I have already told you that I am a bread burner. I usually do not think of cooking bread until the last minute, when it is too late to do the whole thing.

I find that the prepared corn bread mixes are

really very good. And one is about as good as the other. The trick is that you have to add an extra egg or two, depending on how much you are making, and drop a little sugar in there with it—that improves those mixes so that they are just about like regular old homemade corn bread. Put in pork skins and it's Cracklin' Bread. The cheap way.

It's getting pretty confusing to go out and buy bread. There must be about 19,000 different kinds of bread on the market now. There's Fat bread, Skinny bread, Lo-calorie, Hi-calorie, Mrs. So-and-So's bread. Finally, I reached the point of saying— what the hell, then I'll just go back to plain old bread, the kind we had forty years ago. The best, of course, is the bread you bring right out of the oven at home. A lot of the breads that come out of the supermarkets now are not really very good. The kids know best about this. They practically refuse to touch this bread unless it is covered with tons and tons of jelly.

If you make bread at home from a recipe or from a mix, I just have one good solid piece of advice for you. Cook it all the way through. I don't know whether you ever had the experience of biting into a biscuit that was just a little soggy on the inside. That's enough to ruin you for biscuits if you don't know any better. It's just like eating raw dough. My Mama used to wash her strong hands and knead out that dough and make bread in no time at all. You know, it really doesn't cost too much to make bread and it is one of the delights that even poor families can enjoy. Baking is one of the things that I really wish I had learned from Mama. It was like magic when Mama made rolls for Sunday morning. She would put the dough there in the bowl and then cover it over with a wet dish towel and they would rise up. Boy, after that, what else do you need?

I have been experimenting a little bit lately with bread just to see if I can learn a thing or two. One of my experiments turned out very well. I went to the health store and bought some rice flour, and I made some bread with it:

RICE BREAD—
HEALTH-COME-BACK

You put in 2 cups of this special flour, 2 tablespoons of butter, 2 tablespoons of sugar, raisins, 1 egg, or 2 if you like it to be lighter, make the dough, and bake it at 425°. The same bread can be made from white flour, but I think the rice flour makes it something special. This recipe will make about 1 dozen muffins. Those muffins have almost made a bread eater out of me.

I have a few words for you about simplicity at breakfast. For special occasions, when I do have the time to do right by breakfast, there are a few goodies that I honestly enjoy. One is *old-fashioned cheese and eggs;* a lot of people don't know how to fix that. They use the wrong kind of cheese or they put it in there so that it's all lumped up. Mama could do it right and my sisters Virgie and Eura can do it. I'm just getting it. Make no mistake, I am not talking about an omelet, hell no, just eggs and cheese scrambled together so that they blend— so tasty. I use Cheddar, and it's better if the cheese is a little bit sharp so that it won't be blah in the eggs. You want that tangy taste. The thing to do is to get your skillet hot, put the butter in there, then beat your eggs as much as you want to and get them ready to scramble. Grate the amount of cheese that you want ahead of time and add to eggs. Put cheese and eggs in the skillet and cook slowly, stirring constantly. The cheese will melt and mix with the eggs just as the eggs get done, that's the trick. Salt and pepper, and you are in business. Keep stirring *desperately.*

I am not really giving recipes here, just some ideas that you might want to try out for yourself with your own variations. Another delightful breakfast, particularly if you have a little time to get ready, is eggs with green peppers and onions. You chop the green peppers and onions and begin to brown them in a skillet very slowly. Put a little Worcestershire sauce in the eggs and scramble everything together. Good, really good. Here's another goody. Do just about the same thing except add several strips of bacon when you are browning the green peppers and onions. Chop up a couple of hot dogs in there too, then when you add the eggs and scramble, you get everything all mixed up together and it is delicious.

French toast is a good variation and very easy to make. I put the syrup or jam right into the egg mixture before dipping the bread. Potato cakes and eggs provide a very good breakfast, especially if you can afford to have a little piece of meat on the side. Potato cakes are easy. Start with left-over mashed potatoes, molding them into patties. Brown them in butter or bacon grease. If you want them to be extra special, crumble crisp bacon into the potatoes before shaping patties. Sometimes I take scrambled eggs and add rice or left-over hamburger and mix it all up together. Another thing you can do is to take left-over salmon or tuna and throw that in with the eggs. It makes a delicious dish no matter what you think reading this. It may be that the first time the children see this, they will turn up their noses and the second time they are asking for more.

A word about breakfast cereals. How many more of *those* things do you think they are going to put on the market? The other day I must have walked along two full counters. Shelves one on top of the other, row after row, each one of them loaded with different kinds of breakfast cereals. One will make you pop out of bed, one will make you fall out of bed, one will make you skip rope all day, one will give you energy you never had before, one will take off weight, one will add weight if you need it and never had it. I suppose if you kept trying them all, you would find one that would completely destroy you, and one that would make you an absolute love bug all day long, and one that would make hair grow. One that would make your children smile and another one that will make them run away from home. All the while the old oatmeal box is sitting there down at the end, or the cream of farina or Wheatena. They are all still sitting there as good as ever. In my opinion, they are probably the best things on the shelf. People get carried away with new things all of the time. The fact is that all of these fancy new cereals are made by just a few companies. I haven't figured this one out yet. How does a company make something and sell it like hell in order to burn out two or three other products that they are making with the other hand? One day they will praise one cereal to the skies and the next day they will tell you that they have something better. I'll have to ask Mr. Nader or somebody about that. The big issue these days is to get the box with the right toy in it for the kids. Two to one, the toy will be so small that you could eat it up without even realizing it.

SALMON PATTIES

Talking about salmon and eggs made me think of something else tasty. Ahead of time, I will get myself 2 to 4 large cans of salmon (judge by the size of your family). Put the salmon in a bowl, add several eggs, some chopped onions, and salt and pepper. Three or 4 eggs will do it, but if you want more, it won't hurt a thing. Actually, I am pretty extravagant when it comes to eggs and butter. When all of this is mixed up, you roll out the little patties on a plate and stick it in the icebox. Later, when you are ready to cook them, you just lay those things into hot fat, like you would a hamburger, and let them brown on one side, then carefully turn them over. You have to be careful so that they don't fall apart. Some people roll these things in bread crumbs before cooking them.

My main point in this chapter is that Americans lately have gotten pretty fancy in their notions about cooking and everything else. It seems to me it's time for us to start making the move back to simple things where we get honest with ourselves about what is necessary and what is luxury. Simplicity in a way is a luxury; it doesn't deprive anyone. Many of us live in a world in which everybody thinks that a twenty-dollar graduation present is appropriate, but from the *sixth grade?* And we buy that special imported bicycle. . . . Sometimes I think it's mostly so that it could be parked out on the front lawn for all the other children to see, and not so much because it is a very special bicycle when you ride it. Children nowadays feel that they are deprived if they can't get a car when they are sixteen years old. We accept it as normal to have a TV sounding off in every room in the house, especially the children's own room. We really ought to stop and think about what is necessary and what is not.

Dessert, for example, is not necessary. A lot of us seem to think that we have not had a meal unless we have had dessert afterward. Women worry themselves to death, especially when company is coming, thinking, "What will I have for dessert?" I have found out that with my one-pot dinners and with the good basic simple meals, there is no room left for dessert. Maybe at the end of the evening, just as you are beginning to think about going to bed, you might like to have a little nibble on something sweet. Even then, you don't need it. Many days, in our house, we will have breakfast, lunch, dinner, and supper. Supper comes pretty late and it doesn't amount to much—it may be a little sweet or some leftovers. For the occasional dessert or the nighttime snack, I do have a few favorites to pass along to you from a man who is a real master.

SWEET-POTATO PIE
(Billy Wilson)

What's better than the good old-fashioned sweet potato? Mama used to grab sweet potatoes and shove them into the corners of her oven when she was cooking other things. It seemed that she just had to fill up that space. I can't remember a time when she didn't have cooked sweet potatoes on hand. Children are crazy about potatoes. They're good hot or cold. Most of them don't know anything about the yam or sweet potato, but all children like them when they get the chance to taste them. Actually, most youngsters know most about French fried potatoes, those darn things they get in a restaurant. I find that a child usually requires approximately one full bottle of ketchup for a serving of French fries. So even then they are not finding out much about potatoes. Each shoestring gets at least twenty dips of ketchup, which means twenty bites off one slice of potato. I know about this because my Dee Dee is the master of the dip.

Yams and sweet potatoes can be served just as they are cooked, in the skins, but often I like to peel and slice them. Add a bit of brown sugar and some orange juice. It makes them fluffy and light. They are so good cooked this way that they can be used as dessert as well as part of the main meal. Cook covered in the oven at 350°—about 20 minutes if precooked, or 1 hour if raw. Some folks add marshmallows, but I add raisins (cheaper). By the way, yams and sweet potatoes are different colors, so when you're in the market look at the sign. I prefer (if purse says so) yams.

Billy Wilson used to bring food backstage to Lou and me years ago when we worked at the Apollo Theater. He would arrive with his arms loaded with all sorts of homemade delights, enough for everyone to taste a bit. An act of love. And goodness gracious could he cook! Simple things exquisitely prepared. He was best known for his pies. They were unlike any in the world.

One day my accountant and friend, Mr. Nadel, came backstage on business. After trying a piece of pie, he simply hired Billy, who now manages the house and cooks for the Nadels. In this book, Billy is sharing the recipe for two of his pies. Out of *sight* —a moon trip, really!

For sweet-potato pie, boil 5 or 6 sweet potatoes until soft. Rinse in cool water so they will peel easily. After peeling, mash them in a bowl. Add ¾ stick of butter that has been melted with 1 cup of dark brown sugar, 1 teaspoon of nutmeg, 1 teaspoon of vanilla, and ¾ cup of a half-and-half (milk and cream). Add a beaten egg to the mixture, stir into the potatoes, and pour into a pie shell that has been partly cooked. Bake at 350° for 45 minutes or until set.

LEMON CHIFFON PIE
(Billy Wilson)

This makes the filling for 1 9″ pie. Start with 1 envelope plus 1 teaspoon of plain gelatine. Sprinkle it over ¼ cup of orange juice and set the mixture aside to soften. Mix 4 slightly beaten egg yolks with ½ cup granulated sugar, a dash of salt, ½ cup of lemon juice (fresh). Put this mixture into a double boiler to cook until it becomes slightly thickened. Add the softened gelatine and remove from fire. Set aside to cool.

Beat your 4 egg whites until they become foamy. As they are becoming foamy, add ½ cup granulated sugar gradually and continue to whip until they become stiff and smooth and will hold a shape. Gently fold in the cooked egg-yolk mixture and pile it into the pie shell. Put this into the refrigerator for a while. Two hours is enough because it sets very fast.

Before serving, whip ½ pint of heavy cream (add a little vanilla and sugar if desired) and put the whipped cream on top of the pie. Take a fork and make a design in the cream, then cut a slice of lemon peel and curl it on top of the pie.

PIECRUST

(Billy Wilson)

This is for a single 9″ piecrust. You need 1⅓ cups of regular flour, ½ teaspoon of salt, ½ cup plus 2 tablespoons of shortening, and enough water to moisten. Sift flour and salt into a bowl. Add shortening with a fork and knife, blending with the flour until mealy and well mixed. Add just enough water so that the dough will form a ball. Shape it into a ball and roll out on a floured board. Spread it into a pie pan and shape. Prick the dough with a fork and bake at 425° for 10 to 15 minutes, or until it is as brown as you want it to be.

A WINTER FAVORITE DESSERT (Billy Wilson)

Ingredients: 2 cups of flour (self-rising may be used), ½ cup butter, ½ cup sugar, 1 teaspoon vanilla, 1 teaspoon cinnamon, 1 teaspoon nutmeg, ½ teaspoon baking powder (if flour is not self-rising), 2 apples (chopped), milk to moisten (about ½ cup), ½ cup nuts chopped (black walnuts give a fine flavor), and 1 egg.

Cream the butter and sugar, add flour, spices, and baking powder. Beat the egg and add to the mixture. Stir well, moisten with milk, then add nuts and apples and place the mixture into a floured 9¾" square pan. Bake at 350° for 45 minutes.

After eating this, you'll weigh in at 300 pounds, but happily!

CORN PUDDING

Did your mother ever make this? I don't care where you get the corn. Cut it off the cob or use frozen or canned corn (enough for 4 to 6 servings). Add 2 eggs and enough milk (fresh or evaporated) to make it loose. Add salt, a very little bit of pepper to taste, ¼ pound or more of butter, and ¼ to ½ a cup of flour, a taste of vanilla, and a little brown sugar. Mix everything together, cover the pot, and put in a 350° oven for 15 minutes if the corn is precooked or 30 minutes if not. Then uncover and simmer until you see butter around the edges of that

dark top crust. Try some pork chops with this and
see what happens. Excitement prevails.

One of the new things that I have tried is the
juicer. I can recommend it wholeheartedly. Once
in a while they come up with a new contraption that
really makes sense, and this statement comes from
the lady who hasn't come to grips with the toaster
yet. My juicer is one of those like they have at the
health-food store. I drink cucumber juice, which is
supposed to be marvelous for the hair and nails.
With my family I drink carrot juice, great for the
eyes. You would be surprised how good these juices
can be when they are fresh and prepared on one of
these modern juicers. Sometimes I'll mix a little beet
juice in with whatever else I am having and I find
that that is a very good cleanser for the body systems.

I have to tell you a little story about my first experience with that beet juice. I decided that if a little
bit was *good* a lot must be *very good,* so instead of
taking a little shot glass I decided to put mine in a
water glass. Never try that. You will get a body
cleansing all right. In fact, you'll think that someone
has slashed the inside of your body with razor blades.
Stick with the shot glass if you are talking about
pure beet juice.

There is another variation called potassium juice
which has lots of raw vegetable juices. Although
some of the medical authorities are not too sold on
the health-food craze, I really must say that I am.
My first awareness of it was in Las Vegas where I
knew a chorus girl who was really very seriously
ill. It appeared that they were going to have to do
some serious operations on her. She began to drink
fresh juices of all kinds of vegetables and she recovered without any operation at all. She carried
on her dancing career and eventually raised two
children. Believe me, she gave them plenty of
health-food juices.

I enjoy this so much that I might do it even if it
didn't have any healing value. I really do like raw

vegetables. Sometimes I get home from the store and peel a white potato or a sweet potato and eat it raw. Nothing is sweeter or more flavorful. The children are picking up on this fad around the country today. They are very much for being vegetarians and for organic foods, which is another matter altogether. By the way, did you ever try to eat a raw string bean? They are delicious and sweet. Don't just laugh at all of this until you try it.

Contrary to popular belief, it does not take hours and hours of time every day to be a good cook for your family and guests. My life is probably as busy as anyone's, with an office to run, a show-business career to take care of, and a family besides. Yet, honestly, I seldom feel that I am being rushed when it comes to my cooking. Simple cooking is not very time-consuming. It can fit nicely into a day that embraces many other things as well.

I enjoy my days at home when I can do my housecleaning, gardening, handwork (needlepoint, crochet, hooked rugs, embroidery), and cook the meals. With my schedule, I find I need to do a little thinking in advance about how I am going to use time. And I never really let any time go completely empty. It isn't in my nature. I am basically a busy and active person. This is true whether I am on the road or at home. I like to watch a little television, but while watching, I am doing some other things. With a simple routine for your house, there comes a peacefulness, a consistency, a love of what you are doing. There is the joy of accomplishment, the pleasure of feeling that in any given day or any week you have accomplished what you wanted to and have perhaps gone a bit beyond. In the next chapter, I will tell you about a few things I have learned about planning and efficiency. I am no great expert, but I have picked up a few things that might be useful to you.

All Burners On

AVE YOU ever noticed how some women seem to just kill themselves with housework and cooking and yet they never seem to catch up? And then there are other women who keep a good house and cook good meals and never seem to get badly rushed or pressured at any time. As often as not, these women who seem to make it easy also have more outside activities and interests than the woman who stays home and breaks her back. How is this possible?

All women have several roles to fill and some have a great many—housewife, mother, work outside, work inside, and so on. Then some of us also have careers to think about. Under these circumstances it is possible for a woman to get into a trap where she really isn't doing anything very well. That is a shame when it happens, because it makes every day a disappointment and there is a certain feeling of guilt attached to the situation. I figured out a long time ago that if I was going to get to do all the things I wanted to do, which included doing a good job at home for myself and my family, I would have to have my head and hands working on more than one thing at one time. It's almost like cooking on a stove. You know, you can get quite a few things cooked in a short time if you've got all the burners going. Your mind always has a little space to be working on something else that will

61

come later. The key to success, I think, is not to waste any time completely. This doesn't mean that you have to be running around all the time doing four or five things at once. It means that you are *doing* things instead of sitting on your fanny *thinking* about them. While you are going about your business, you are thinking about some of your other responsibilities and how you are going to take care of them. I don't offer myself as a big expert on efficiency, but my life has been such that I have had to find a few ways to conserve time and get a lot of things done. That's what this chapter is about.

Sometimes, even with good planning, you need a meal in a hurry. I had some pretty good examples early in my life, because my Mama was the fastest cook in the East, a real shotgun cooker as I've told you She could get cabbage on the table before we could get the knives and forks put around. She'd say, "Set the table," and it seems to me that by the time we got that straight, she had the food sitting there steaming on the table.

MAMA'S CABBAGE

Mama always quartered a cabbage. She put it into about ¼ pan of water and boiled it *without a top.* In the water, use a small piece of bacon (or some bacon grease), or some ham or salt pork.

For smothered cabbage, cook it like greens in plain water until *almost* done. In a frying pan, cook bacon or salt pork, then add the cabbage and a little water. Cover and simmer until done. Yum!

One of the things she taught me should be obvious to everyone, but I still find a lot of cooks who haven't figured it out yet. Put the food on first that takes the longest to cook. Nothing is more exasperating than going to someone's home for dinner, "at six sharp" according to the hostess, only to find dinner not started. Then she starts off by making the salad. Oh, Lawdy! I do some of the time-consuming things ahead of time. That way, I can put a meal on the table in about 20 to 30 minutes. If I know that I'm going to be extra busy the next night, I'll just double up in the oven and do a little cooking in advance.

Because in my business I'm away a lot, I cook a lot of things in advance and put them in the freezer. I start to double up on the amount of food I put in the oven each time I cook, so that in three or four days I can prepare a half freezer full of food to leave behind for the family. On such occasions I have often cooked four or five roasts at once, then prepared a lot of spaghetti sauce and let everything cool overnight. The next morning I package things up and put them into the freezer. Then all that has to be done later is to get them out and thaw them, heat, and serve. A roast is better if you cook it only three quarters of the regular ·time before freezing, and put some juice in the freezer package.

I save myself a little time before I ever leave the grocery store. While the cashier is checking me out, I separate all the things I mean to cook that day. Those go into a separate bag. That way, when I hit the door and the kids come out to help me grab all those bags of groceries, I don't have to waste a lot of time looking for the pork chops or the rice or trying to see what happened to the steak I bought.

I find that I do usually arrive at home just about the time I should be starting to cook, so that means that I have no time to waste, and, believe me, I'm thinking about that in the car as I drive up to the house. I come to the door with my hat on, but the first think I do is kick off my shoes. Then I actually start my meal by going into that bag that has the number-one priority items in it. As soon as I've got something going, preferably the longest cooking item, I go back and start unpacking and storing all the rest of the groceries. That way, I really haven't wasted any time at all. Just think how much longer it would take me if I came in and decided to put everything away, and then had to find the things that I needed for that particular meal, and then started cooking. It would take me a good thirty or forty minutes longer to get dinner on the table.

And you know what? Time and time again I have found myself standing at the stove cooking away and humming and singing with that hat still on my head. I don't know what it is, I guess in thinking so intently about getting my meal started, I forget about everything else. It doesn't hurt the taste of the food though.

I am not a dainty and precise cook. I enjoy moving those pots and pans around, and I get a certain pleasure from putting a meal together quickly and with very little wasted time and motion. One of my dearest friends, Peetny Redman, represents just the other extreme. Peetny is a very delicate and dainty little rose of a woman. The difference between us shows up in everything pertaining to the kitchen. For example, Peetny is a delicate table setter. She will take all the pains in the world to arrange a centerpiece just so with each rose bending its head in the right direction. Where she uses a rose centerpiece, I use a food centerpiece. I usually don't bother with a real centerpiece at all. I actually find it distracting even in restaurants to be trying to talk to someone while looking through flowers that sit between us.

Peetny chops each carrot just so; she can lay out a piece of celery so carefully you'd think it was a wake. She's a terrific cook, but the style is entirely different. Hers is prettier.

I don't like to make a big deal about cooking. After all, I like to enjoy other activities around the house with my family. I definitely do not like to stop and say, "Well, now I must prepare dinner." Actually, it's a strange way I cook. I just disappear. I might be outdoors cutting the roses and I'll step inside as if to get something. While I'm in there, the cooking action may start.

On occasions, I have had the pork chops all ready and I've decided that that's really not what I want to cook and serve. On the stage I keep my hand on the pulse of the audience; in the kitchen,

I measure the pulse of the family. Honey, it's perfectly all right to set the chops aside for another time. Maybe I decide what would really be good and what everyone would enjoy the most is liver. Quite a few things run through Pearlie Mae's mind while she's cooking or cleaning. I always have music going, so I'll hear something I like and, wow, it comes! I may just step over to the phone and call my arranger and say, "Hey, I just heard this crazy song." I don't make a big deal out of getting ready for a show, and I don't make a big deal about getting ready for a meal. I find that if I keep everything warm, with all burners on, all I have to do is turn the right burner up when the time comes and I am ready to go.

I mentioned going to the grocery store. You know, there are many women who wind up going to the store just about every day. They'll get started on something in the kitchen and then realize that they don't have one of the ingredients, or maybe they will run out of some basic thing like bread and have to go back. Not me. I don't particularly enjoy going to the grocery store, so I do it as seldom as possible. This means that when I go, I have to get everything. Don't forget, I use my freezer, so I am able to store a great many things for use later on. But I have no idea how many hundreds of hours I have saved by doing one big shopping maybe once every month or six weeks. In-between, when the urge strikes you, you can once in a while pick up something in the way of fresh fruit and vegetables, but you don't have to do that very often either. Just think of the gasoline you can spend going to the store because you run out of salt and pepper.

I go overboard on that one. You will always find twelve boxes of pepper and twelve boxes of salt in my house. When I was little, my Mama read the Bible where it said that salt is the savor of the earth, and she realized that it was important not to run out of these important commodities. The fact is that it represented a kind of security to provide for us in that way by having some salt and pepper stored. Long before the Second World War struck, Mama seemed to anticipate that there would be shortages on things that we liked and needed very much. It was as if she saw the ghost of war coming on. Mama was born with a veil over her face, by the way, and I do think that in some ways she had the powers that are supposed to go with that. The same thing applied to sugar. She started to store it. Mama put sugar in big lard cans, and I do that now too. Mama's sugar got so hard you could take an ax and hit it. When the war struck, everyone was drinking coffee without sugar, or they were crying for a little more in their ration books. Mrs. Bailey's children were drinking lemonade loaded with sugar during the war. Actually, Mama had been stockpiling sugar for at least two or three years before anybody realized that a war was about to happen. I suppose that now the storehouse of salt and pepper and sugar that I have at home is some kind of symbolic security for me.

Sometimes in my late-night working and thinking in the kitchen, I'll decide I want a little something good to eat. Do you know just how simple that could be? I get a lot of pleasure out of a piece of bread with cheese melted on top. Put cheese on top of bread. Load it up. Lay it on foil and put it under the broiler. Put a cup of coffee with that and one couldn't want much more for a late-night snack.

It is during these late hours that I do a lot of my thinking ahead. One night, I made good use of several hours in the kitchen. I knew that the next day I had to get my meals fixed and make a trip for a fitting of dresses for a London appearance and a Flip Wilson Show, both coming up very quickly. I had to get down to the passport office too. Thinking of all this driving naturally made me realize that the car was past due for some new tires. So I would try for that on my travels. In addition to these things, I knew that I wanted to work with my nieces on their hooked rugs. Oh yes, I had to stop by my office to take care of some business. In the back of my mind was a piece of needlepoint that I had been wanting to get back to for days and days. Tomorrow I would have to do at least a little of that. Then too, because of my need for exercise and an increase in my strength, I meant to spend an hour and a half to two hours at the pool, and a good deal of that time I would actually be swimming for the exercise. Even as I was trying to sort out all of these pieces and figure how I was going to do all of this and still get the meals prepared, I was thinking of what I would like to do most on the Flip Wilson Show.

Actually, as the day worked out, it was no particular sweat. I stayed in the kitchen until almost three o'clock in the morning. You have nights like that when it seems a shame to go to sleep. Finally, I just lay down on the floor there as I do quite often, and I dozed off. Louis found me there in the morning and fortunately wasn't alarmed because he had seen that happen before. I sleep very well on the kitchen floor.

I figured I had to leave home by eight-thirty in the morning in order to get my morning rounds done. As I cooked breakfast and as we ate it, I was cooking part of dinner—things that I could shove away into the icebox until the right time. After dinner that night, with all of my chores accomplished, I really felt that I had made the most of the day. That is a good feeling.

Even if I had time, I don't think I could make myself slice butter into a pot. A lot of cooks slice the butter. That just doesn't make any sense to me. In fact, I'm really not all that careful. I've tried it, but I find it just too hard to stick to a certain way of putting a dinner together. I know that when butter goes into the pot, it is going to melt, so why slice?

I have a neighbor who is very meticulous about following her recipes. Everything is just so. One time I got one of her recipes and I was going to try to follow it word for word, letter for letter. I mean I got out my measuring cups and measuring spoons, I even got out the thing you use to measure water, and I put on an apron and a chef's hat. Really! Well sir, I went through a couple of items with the spoons and then I measured a cup of flour and it didn't look like enough to me. That did it. The next thing I knew, I forgot all about the recipe and I reached over and got my coffee cup, dipped it into the flour barrel and measured it out that way.

In a way, that is similar to my approach to living. We don't live our lives in *quantity*. Life is *quality*, and you don't measure that precisely by the cup. Recipes, to me, are often wrong when they tell you how many people they will serve. As soon as I get a recipe that says it will serve six, it turns out that it is not enough because it's so good, or else I've got too much because I screwed it up somehow. How do we know anyway how much any one person is going to eat? I don't like the idea, when I am cooking, of having to stop and get out my little measuring cup in my mind and say that this is how much one person will eat and this is how much that other person will eat. So I just cook. When I cook, I generally like to have some food left over. Same thing with life, right?

BAKED SOLE SPONTANEOUS

I am going to use this recipe just to show you how to let yourself go when you are cooking. You can improvise sometimes and do some things that are very nice. There's a pleasure in it. Recently, I threw this sole in the oven at 350° with butter, salt, and pepper on it and just a touch of garlic. I like to bake fish because the juices seem to stay there more so than with broiling. Broiling, it seems to me, often dries out the meat in a fish. Just about the time I closed the oven door, I had this weird idea. I hauled that sole out of there again, sprinkled it with a little Accent and sprinkled Parmesan cheese over the top of it. Tangy and tasty to a tee. I served cabbage and rice with it and the whole family had a real ball.

WHITEFISH
AND RED SNAPPER

Use about equal parts of each one. With a little hot water, mix 1 bouillon cube, parsley. Add a little onion, green pepper, garlic, oil, salt, and pepper. Seal each piece of fish into a heavy piece of metal foil. Put it into a hot oven or over a good barbecue fire. Louis makes a fire for me, and that could be another book! After about 15 minutes, depending on how hot the fire is, open the foil a little bit and add some soy sauce, close it back up and let it cook just a bit longer. When you open it up and serve it, all those flavors have mixed and the fish is very moist and delicious.

From all I have said about fudging on recipes and improvising as you go along, and from my remarks about cooking a meal in a hurry, you might think that I am a fairly slam-bang, careless person in the kitchen. That is not true, because I know that the kitchen can be a haven or it can be a disaster area if you get careless in there.

Stop and think about it. There are many dangers possible in the kitchen. A lot of women wear flowing caftans or robes that have ruffled puffs. They come into the the kitchen in the morning to fix breakfast and they may be in a little bit of a hurry. As soon as they turn on a gas burner, they are courting a long stay in the hospital or perhaps death if they are not careful. Those flames jump way up there from a gas burner when you first turn it on and some of the material that these clothes are made out of will go up pretty fast. It isn't worth going up in flames to prove how gorgeous you can look. Be neat in the kitchen, but not a fashion model. You may be a divine-looking creature, but that won't matter if the old man has to call the fire department instead of eating his eggs.

Funny thing is, it also scares my son, Tony. I

think he must have realized the danger from watching me when I am around fire. If anything, Tony is overly careful. Even if he decides to light a lady's cigarette, when he strikes the match he reacts as if he were carrying the Olympic torch between his fingers. If a match flares up more than usual, Tony will drop it or throw it away. Of course that sets me off to screaming, because two to one he has thrown it down on a rug somewhere. He has a real thing for flames.

I was careful to teach my children the safe way of lighting a gas stove. Many people turn on the gas before they even have a match in hand! It's worse with the oven—you know, they have the gas on for a few seconds, then lean down with their head practically inside and strike a match. Pop goes the weasel!

Anyway, we were talking about safety in the kitchen. Isn't it funny how a mother can find some excuse to start talking about her children! What do you have in your kitchen to help when you want to reach something that is a little too high? I think it is important to have a really good stool or maybe just a good firm wooden box around the kitchen. Climb up on it and get your feet set before you start reaching over your head for something in the cabinet. It can be disconcerting at the very least to have seventeen cans of something come down on your head while you are trying to cook a meal.

A little stretching and bending here and there can be good for your waistline if you do it right. Most of the exercise in our kitchens is fading away these days. For example, nobody uses those old-fashioned can openers any more. The ones where you had a little wrist action going for you. Now everybody, including me, has some kind of electric can opener. They are marvelous when they are working and they are a horror when they *don't* work. The worst kind of electric can opener is the one that *sort* of works, if you know what I mean. You think the top is cut out, but it isn't really, so you start slipping things under the edge to see if you can help it along a little bit and two to one you are going to cut part of your finger off.

You have to use your head all the time in the kitchen. It takes a certain amount of thinking just to get a meal on the table with everything hot. Even if you make it, you still have to get the gang seated before things get cold. Still, along the way, you have to remember not to leave the pan handle sticking out where you can run into it, or, worse still, your child can reach up and turn something over on his head. You have to watch that with knives when you leave them sticking over the edge of a counter or leave the point sticking up in a drainer or open dishwasher. A wet place on the floor—you can forget that in two seconds flat when you are busy, turn around and fall flat on your forgetfulness. If you drop something on the floor and glass flies everywhere, stop and take the time to find every bit of it. Wet a paper towel or a cloth and run it over that floor with your hand if necessary until you get every one of those little shiny things up off the floor. This is especially important if you cook barefoot the way I do. A lot of women refuse to form the habit of using a cutting board in the kitchen when they are slicing or dicing things. It's good to use a chopping block, because it can save you that one time when you might cut your thumb. You know how a lot of women will stand there and scrape something by pulling a knife toward the stomach. Once in a while it will get you. It isn't worth it. Mary Fairbanks (wife of Douglas Fairbanks, Jr.) just recently had a wild thing happen. She was trying to get the lid off a tin cake-box, and she did just what you and I do. She hugged it to her body and pulled hard at the far edge. Suddenly, the top came off and her arm flew back. Mary cracked a rib. Think about that next time you start to tug!

The oven is a bad spot too, even apart from lighting it. You ought to make the children, who are naturally interested, stand completely away or leave the kitchen altogether when you open up an oven, because the first thing you are going to do is to grab something hot and heavy and turn around with it. Even if you don't bump the kids, they may still reach a hand in there to do what you did. Children are great imitators of what they see. If you get any kind of a little burn you can take a lot of the fire out of it by putting it immediately into ice-cold water. Immerse it completely and drop a couple of cubes in there if necessary to keep it really cold. Five or ten minutes of that and you could save yourself some of the grief that goes along with the burn. The main thing is that whatever you are doing in the kitchen, you should be thinking about the possible dangers involved. Form good habits and make no exceptions.

For most women, holiday time really taxes efficiency in the kitchen. Actually, my cooking habits don't change much at all for holidays. Probably, I will have a few more people around and so I'll increase the quantities of everything when I·cook. When I fire up my ovens, and I have two, I make sure that I get the full benefit of every inch of space in both of them. It isn't unusual at holiday time for me to be cooking a turkey, a ham, and a loin of pork, and sometimes I cook more than one of each. I let myself be governed mostly by how much room I have left in the top or in the bottom. Meanwhile, on the burners, I've got string beans, broccoli, and always buttered rice. It's not that I intend to serve all these things at once, it's just that I know that I don't want to make a great big production out of every mealtime during a holiday season. I fix it so that I have a little head start on things.

Cooking is not drudgery for me, *any time*. During the festive seasons, I love to keep my house full of good smells. I like to spread the finest table that my pocketbook will allow. It gets back to my feeling about the kitchen and food as a way of sharing and giving. Holidays simply provide me with a larger challenge than regular days provide. I know that if I could do a good job of it on those days, that

that is a thing to be proud of. My feast comes in the preparation; my gift, in the anticipation of everyone's enjoyment. I like to have that holiday seasonal music playing on the radio and smell the mixture of delicious aromas. I like to conjure in my imagination the quality of the meals I want to serve. Then I like to give the task my full attention. I get my brain going in three or four channels at once. I turn on all the burners and hold nothing back.

I Don't Iron Dust Rags

Y MAMA DID. I guess she ironed every dust rag she ever had, and she didn't let them get very dirty either. She would use them about once or twice and then put them in the wash. Mama was just about the most thorough and dedicated housekeeper I have ever seen in my life. In fact, if I tell you the truth, I have to say that she actually went overboard. Mama's *life* was in that house. It was her castle—the place to show how well she could do things. She left no corner, no crack, no tiny spot untouched when she cleaned house. I had Mama in a hotel once and she insisted on remaking the beds her way, even though they looked pretty good to me in the first place.

When I was just a little girl, Mama showed me how well it could be done. I learned to appreciate a neat and clean house. I learned that to have a house like that required the co-operation of everybody in the family. Mama ruled our roost, and every one of us had a certain responsibility for helping to keep it the way Mama wanted it to be. The technique was there, that steady alertness that you have to have if you are going to be a good housekeeper. I didn't bring away all of Mama's habits, but I brought away a certain attitude and a certain technique for dealing with housework. There are a great many women in the world who will try to keep a clean house but never seem to catch up. You can't do it all at once.

Why do a complete spring housecleaning once a week? Instead, have a system that keeps each member of the house doing housework as a regular part of *living* in the house. It means that you have to delegate responsibilities to the other people who live there. They have to be habitual housecleaners as well as you. This doesn't mean that everybody has to be enslaved by housework. It just means that without really thinking about it too much, one can do a lot of the little things that make a difference.

The first house that Louis and I owned presented a few challenges for me. Come to think of it, getting in there provided a few challenges for Louis too, because at the time we were married, he was just a little more fragile than I was. Carrying me across the threshold was completely out of the question, because I had a little weight on at the time.

I didn't get to look at that house before Louis bought it; he thought it would be fun to surprise me with it. What he surprised me with was a charming house as you looked at it from the outside, but inside it had a tiny, tiny kitchen and practically no closets at all. Isn't that like a man to forget about those things? By the way, the house had no heat, either! Of course, we did live in California, but I still like to have that warmth in the house. I am just cold-natured, I guess. I remember being in Duluth, Minnesota, one time, which, I guess, is the coldest place I've ever been. It was forty degrees below zero. I landed at the airport and got a cab to the hotel. I was going to do a concert the next night. All the way in from the airport, I kept swearing that I really wasn't cold. But when I got into the hotel lobby, I suddenly had an awful feeling. My clothes had sort of frozen, and I felt as I stood there exactly as if I had gone to the bathroom like a little kid right there in the lobby. It was the strangest feeling, and if you've ever had it, you'll know exactly what I mean.

Anyway, Louis pointed out that the house did have a fireplace. I said, "Fine, Honey, but where's the furnace?" He had to admit that there was none.

We had to have a heater installed. Well, by the time that thing came I already had the drapes hung. The men said they were going to have to cut some vents in here and there. That meant that the drapes had to come down and they had to be cut off. You know how much I liked Louis at that moment. It took me quite a while to get a routine established at that house, believe me.

I like to clean a house before I move into it. I don't care how clean it looks, I still find that I could do a little good in there before the rugs and furniture arrive. There's an old wives' tale that I follow—I don't know why—to the effect that when you move into a new house, you are supposed to go in with a broom and a box of salt and leave them in the empty house before you put any furniture or anything in it. It's just that when I go in there with the salt, I also move that broom around a little bit and take me some rags and clean the place up. I do a little housecleaning even in hotel rooms, where I live a lot of the time. I have to treat a hotel like I treat my home. When the children go on the road with me, I insist that they make their own beds, just to keep in the habit. The maid always says, "Well, I'm supposed to do that." I tell her, "Yes, but they don't have any money. They didn't pay for this room. They make their beds at home and I don't want them to forget how it is done." Everywhere we go, my children respect the furnishings and the property of others.

I remember that when I was a tiny girl we left Washington, D.C., to move to Philadelphia. My Mama, tired as she was from packing, took some extra hours and cleaned that empty house from stem to stern. I said, "Mama, what's this all about? We are moving out, aren't we?" She said, "Yes, but when the next people come in I don't want them to think I'm a dirty woman." She left that empty house spotless. I think that's a pretty good practice. You know, when some people move out of a place, an apartment or a house, they leave a pretty depressing sight for the people who are moving in. I have never left a place dirty in my life.

I have said that in a way my kitchen is a sanctuary for me. It is a place where I feel comfortable. To some degree, that extends to my whole house. When I am at home and have the feeling of being comfortable and relaxed, it is very difficult to get me out of there. Maybe I got some of that from Mama too. Make no mistake about it, once I get out for a party or an evening, I can have a ball and I can stay out for a long time. The difficult part is to get me out of the house in the first place.

I am the same way about hotel rooms when I am on the road and in a town where I have work. Not too long ago, I played the Americana in New York. I was there for five weeks in all on a job that lasted three weeks and five days. During that time, I didn't go out. I worked downstairs in The Royal Box and I stayed in my room and did handcrafts and watched TV and wrote letters and made notes for this book. There is nothing that relaxes me more than turning on the radio for some good music or flipping on a ball game on TV and sitting there with my shoes off and crocheting. Remember, when I step out on the street, I sometimes find myself surrounded. There really isn't too much difference between being onstage and being on the street. People simply know who I am. When I am out among people, I just automatically give everything I've got. When I am in my room or in my house, I am a complete loner. I am a very poor one for having a lot of visitors. I don't drop in on friends and I have the type of friends who don't do it to me either. That's marvelous as far as I'm concerned. When we see each other we enjoy it, but we see each other by mutual consent and agreement, with love.

That goes for my neighbors too. I have lived in the same neighborhood now for almost eight years. I nod to my neighbors and they nod to me. We know that if either of us needs the other, help will be forthcoming. I am not the least bit interested in what my neighbor is doing in his yard, and

I don't think he should be too interested in what I am doing in mine. There is a line that I don't want to cross. I don't want to get to the point where we are borrowing sugar every day and dropping in back and forth for coffee and gossip, because it is possible to get too chummy, so that people become a drain on one another. Apart from my personality reasons, there are practical reasons why I don't like a lot of chumminess. I can't get my cooking and housecleaning done when I am at home if I have constant distractions. Girl friends who sit around running off at the mouth all day are really copping out on the things that they are supposed to be doing well. I suppose the women's lib people wouldn't care for that too much, but it is honestly my opinion.

Taking care of my house, my family, my kitchen, and my career keeps me cooking on all burners as it is. I keep my mind active around the house, and I do it without any great amount of tension or nervousness. I intend to keep it that way. I live quietly around my house with great enjoyment, but I carry a big stick. I just don't like to have my solitude and my routine interrupted, because they mean a great deal to me. I like the feeling that comes from jumping out of the pool to go start some rice because it just crossed my mind that Tony wants some rice pudding. I am a loner, but the others I love lie dormant in me somewhere all the time. The wishes of others enter me and I move to fulfill them.

God gives each of us a stove. Some people light one burner at a time, and thus slow down on their cooking and on their lives. God gave me a stove and said to me, "Cook on it." He did not tell me what to cook or how much. My feeling is that I must keep that stove forever warm, and that for as long as it is possible for me to do so, I should keep all the burners lighted. My physicians have told me on occasion to turn my stove down a bit for my own good. I know, without having to think about it, that for me it would be a mistake to turn things down too much. I cannot let myself go cold to humanity, cold to everything but Pearl. My doctors can't see it, but I know if I turn my stove down to a certain degree, it will go completely cold. I will not exist. I will die. In the hospital, on one occasion I ceased to breathe. I have been that close, and somehow in that experience I found courage.

I can turn things down a bit without turning off any burners altogether. The way I live now makes me think of something Louis did a few weeks ago. We got to bed late knowing that we had to get up early to catch a plane the next morning. About six o'clock I got up to put some coffee on so that we could have it before we left for the airport. As I rounded the corner to the kitchen, I smelled coffee. I was puzzled. It turned out that Louis, thoughtful man that he is, had set the coffee up and put it over a very, very low flame. That coffee was just right for pouring. You don't have to boil, you can simmer.

The big task for me, the thing that has been hardest for me to learn, is to strike the moderate pace without stopping. I have had to find the balance between the automatic thing for me, which is to give all I have to anyone who needs me, and the *un*natural thing for me, which is to feel concerned for the selfish aspects of survival. I guess I know that if I kept all my burners as hot as they would go, if I yielded to the automatic impulse to give all that I have, I would ultimately be left with nothing but death. Over and over again through the years, Louis has tried to reason with me about this. He has pointed out to me that I didn't seem to know how to be selfish, even when it was wise to be selfish for my own sake and my own survival. At this point, I really don't know whether I am talking about a fault or a virtue in myself over the years. I do know that repeatedly it has brought me near the point of death. Today, I know who Pearl is as *Pearl* knows. I do not know the Pearl that *other* people *say* she is.

Over and over again through the years, I have parted with friends who refused to see the difference between the usual stereotype of a show-business celebrity and the real person. I find that for me friendships endure only when people get to know me as an individual, and forget about all the expectations they have of a show-business headliner. I don't necessarily conform to the usual show-business pattern.

A show is a show and it is constructed to be as pleasant as possible. One time I came through a dispute with a person who worked with me, someone who had been a friend of mine for a long time. This person said, "You're being so tough and demanding offstage, but I never saw these feelings come out when you were working onstage." I guess the person was implying a kind of two-faced behavior on my part. I said, "Listen, the reason you haven't seen those emotions onstage is that you haven't *interrupted* me and *bothered* me on*stage.* If you had ever done that, you would see exactly the same feelings coming out there as are coming out now." What they really wanted was me doing a continuous stage show.

Think about it. You know that a show-business personality has to be basically a human being, whether he is on the stage or off the stage. People get an image of us on the stage when we are doing carefully constructed routines—when we are happy-go-lucky and everything is sunlight and daffodils. It isn't fair to hold the same expectations of me when I walk off the stage. I'm the same person all right, but the circumstances are different. If I could have one wish fulfilled, I guess it would be that people, even strangers, would respond to me on the street in a different way than they respond to me on the stage. I don't *always* mind to stop and talk and shake hands and sign autographs, but *sometimes* I do. There's a resentment that comes into me when I realize that my life is controlled by an image that people have built. I know that on those occasions when I don't have time to stop because I'm in pursuit of my personal life, people turn and say something snide about me. It is as if performers did not have the right to private lives. When I got out of the hospital this most recent time, I had a very sore arm, because of a catheterization for the heart problem. That's the deal where they stick a tube in your arm and run it all the way up to your heart. I don't suppose it had anything to do with the treatment, but I also had tendonitis and a stiff neck. I was sleeping in a neck brace at night and doing everything I could during the day to ease the pain in my arm. At night I was doing two shows on the stage. My arm finally got so bad that I couldn't put my hand on my hip. I was feeling like holy hell. Well, no matter how you're feeling, you still have to get from the hotel to the stage, and to do that you still have to pass by people. It seemed to me that during that bad time everybody who saw me wanted to grab me by the arm. I found myself absolutely jumping away from people. Then, as often as not, I would turn to look back over my shoulder and try to explain to people what was the matter, because I figured I might have hurt their feelings. I thought about putting one arm in a sling, but actually both of them were sore. That would have been too much, carrying both arms around in slings. The minute someone would say "I'm sorry," it made me sad. I couldn't seem to win.

Now that I have gone through all of that with you, maybe you will understand a bit more about my attitude toward my house as a place of privacy and cleanliness and solitude. I don't keep a clean house because I have people running in and out of there. I keep it because *I* want it that way and because, in a way, it is the most important place in my life. In the way that I am speaking of it, it is more important than the most exotic foreign country. It is more important than the stage even. It is the place where I keep in touch with *me* without the interruptions of images and the claims of other people upon me. I am speaking, of course, of people outside my family, for the members of my family are truly part of myself.

I am trying to pass along to my children the

belief that they should take pride in their house just because it is their place. If the children do the dishes and I inspect the glasses afterward and find that they haven't done a thorough job, I bring them back to it and show them that doing a job well is worthwhile in itself. If I reach under the counter for a pot and put my hand on a little greasy spot, that finishes me. I have sat in one too many restaurants along the road and found greasy silverware or dirty dishes put in front of me. I don't have fancy pans in my kitchen, but I have clean ones.

My favorite pans were given to me when I was in *Porgy and Bess.* I turned forty, and one of the top men of the staff gave me a whole set of frying pans. I took them home to Apple Valley and I have been using them ever since. They ranged from a thing that would practically cover the whole top of the stove down to a little teeny-weeny thing for one egg.

They've got this new thing out, the frying pan that nothing will stick to. The only trouble with those things is that they are not heavy enough. I think they are made of aluminum, and that is not a frying pan. The old heavy frying pan holds heat better, and they cook food evenly and slowly. I don't care for the pressure cooker either. I know what they are supposed to do—they can cut the cooking time down to practically nothing. Part of my trouble is that I saw one of those pressure cookers *blow* one time. They can actually cook your food to shreds even when you use them correctly. Maybe I am not being fair. Perhaps it is just that I never learned the technique; I figure that food should have a little time to live, and somewhere in the back of my mind I always have the image of that darn thing blowing up in my face. It makes me jittery just having it there.

We may as well admit that some of our reactions are not entirely rational. I guess I am that way about gas cooking. I don't like electric stoves. I can't find a good reason for it. I mean, I know that gas can blow you away the same as electricity can kill you. Even the old wood stove, if you didn't start it off right, could make a pretty bad mess of things. It just seems to me that I can regulate the gas better. Electricity gets rolling along a little too fast for me. I keep thinking what's going to happen when the pot boils over and that water hits the coils. It wouldn't happen, I guess, but I keep thinking about that electricity mixing with that water.

Mama kept her gas stove immaculately clean. After she got through cooking, it wasn't enough to just wipe off the top. You had to get a clean rag and really polish it so that everything was shiny. That went for all the chrome in the kitchen. There was no such thing as a water faucet with spots on it. Mama kept those things polished. Whenever she got ready to walk out of the kitchen, she would just take a rag and shine up the front of the icebox.

I'll talk more about teaching children about housework later on. For now, just let me say I think it is very sad in America to see young girls who aren't taught to cook and keep house. There's a time to learn that. The only thing a lot of youngsters know now is how to prepare hot dogs and hamburgers. Where does that leave them if they have to do for themselves in an emergency? Or maybe it's just a case where Mother is at work. There's one hopeful sign though. Some of the kids are interested in returning to nature. Even in the communes they learn to cook, and they learn to do it simply. They are camping out and traveling around and getting it all together. They are eating natural foods, and digging herbs and putting together weird dishes. Regardless of what you think about some of the things they do, they are getting back to some honesty with their food.

One thing is for sure—when the rest of the family knows a little something about cooking and keeping house, it can help the lady of the house quite a bit. Louis is a tremendous help to me—he's a very neat and particular person. If he steps over to the sink to get a glass of water and sees a stain there, nine times out of ten he will pick up a paper towel and just polish it off. Like mine, his whole family was like that. Louis protects our house like a mother hen, and when something is wrong he likes to have it fixed completely and immediately. If there is a nail out of place, Louis cannot be satisfied until it is nailed in. It almost becomes a big deal with him if the side of the house looks dirty. I might say, "Well, we can hose it down, wash it real good, and then maybe in about six months we'll put aside some money and have it painted." I can remember one case in which after saying something like that I went off to do a job. Louis stayed at home. When I got back a little over a week later, we had a different color house. He had had the whole thing done. If we notice a little crack in the sink, I say, "Well, we'll get a little patch for that." Louis would rather have a whole new sink. He can't stand to have anything fall apart. He functions by the moment, and that's different from me. I may look like I am never going to get something done, and then in one hour, when you least expect it, I'll do twenty things.

Of course, the main trick is to keep the big jobs from coming up too often. One of the big ones that we all hate is oven cleaning. On the market these days they have every kind of oven cleaner in the world, and each one, they say, is better than the other. If you can believe what you see on TV, all you have to do is spray that stuff on there, then go away and do a little light housework somewhere and step back in and finish it off. That's not so, particularly if your oven really and truly needs cleaning.

There are some things that you know will make a mess when you put them in the oven. You know it even before you get started. One of them is sweet potatoes. I've told you that if there is any vacant space left in my oven when I start cooking, I'm apt to shove something in the corner. Sweet potatoes are a natural; they'll fit in anywhere. As sure as you do this, you are liable to let those potatoes cook just a little too long. If you do, they are going to pop and the sweet juice is going to run out into the oven. That makes a very hard oven-cleaning job, so I prevent it. I simply put a little piece of metal foil under each potato. Then if it pops, I have no problem anyway.

You may not have ever thought of it this way, but housework can be a superior form of exercise. All my life until recently I enjoyed the physical workout that you get cleaning house. Then, with my recent heart attack, the doctors said, "No more." The thing that bothered them a little was the fact that you do a lot of reaching over your head, and they find that to be straining on the heart muscles. If you are in basic good health, housework can be one of the greatest exercises in the world. It is a practical exercise and it can be done with love. If you insist on making a chore out of housework or anything else, it can be a real disaster. If you keep yourself alive and active and interested in many things at once, including keeping a good house, you can relax and live to be a hot hundred years old and still end up a size twelve. With all that and doing all the work that you do, you would still be able to throw in one hard kick at the end of each evening.

Speaking of size twelve, I believe that fasting has a real positive value for people. The comedian Dick Gregory has been on a fast of liquids for a very, very long time now, as I write this. He has gone down to eighty-five pounds, and I would say that that is carrying things a bit too far. His fast, of course, is a public protest. Fasting for shorter periods than that is actually a Biblical thing, and I do believe it can be good for you physically. It leads to meditation, and somehow it seems to cleanse your soul and your body. If you make it through one day of fasting, you can make it through two. For two or three days, I will simply eat nothing until six o'clock at night. It seems to leave my body completely free. Of course, just to keep myself from getting into some deep trouble, I ought to tell you that your doctor should give the go-ahead before you try it. That way, you see, if you are not able to take it, you can't come back to me and blame me for anything bad that happens to you. Anyway, learning to see what needs to be done—that's half the battle. It doesn't seem to come naturally to some people. They can look around a room without noticing the things that are wrong with it. Mama taught me and I have been trying to teach my children. So far, I think they are doing pretty well. When they miss the boat, I let them know it right away. With my nieces and my daughter around the house all summer, I have had a chance to do some fairly intensive teaching. The other day I stepped into the kitchen in the middle of the afternoon and started to open the icebox. I grabbed the handle and couldn't let it go because there was something sticky on there. I forgot all about getting my drink of water. I just turned right around, stepped out to the swimming pool and I found my dishwasher from noontime. I said, "All right, young lady, out, right now, out of the pool!" She had to dry off and go inside and polish the front of the icebox. After a few times, I think she'll remember that she's responsible for checking everything before she checks out. I didn't let it stop there. I asked those little girls what kind of jelly they had had and they looked at each other as if to say, "How did dear old Aunt Pearl know we had jelly at all?" I said, "I know very well you had jelly because you took it out of the icebox and then you didn't wash your hands. And when you put it back, you left it on the front of the handle. Now I'll make you a bet. I'll bet that if I look inside the icebox, I'll find that the jelly is on the outside of the jar as well as on the inside. What do you think?" They just stood there. So I reached in the icebox and sure enough that darn jar was sticky all over. They had to wash that too before they could get back to their play. I have visited in many supposedly well-kept homes where nobody apparently wiped around the top of the jar before putting the lid back on. The result is that there's all that dried-up sticky stuff around the top of the jelly, the syrup, the peanut butter, and so on. It makes me kind of sick.

I just know that those are the same houses where they have that magic drawer full of recipes, match-books, broken electrical sockets, screws that don't fit anything, and other junk. They know and I know that they are not ever going back into the drawer for a broken pencil, a five-year-old receipt, or a piece of cord six inches long.

I am particular about how the drawers are kept in my house. No problem with Louis, as you might expect. He can put his hand into his dresser and get what he wants without even looking. Every sock is in its place. In fact, when he puts pencils or a pack of chewing gum on his dresser at night, he lines everything up in a row. You could look again two years later and still find those same things lined up in the same order—it never varies. Our kids are supposed to keep ther own rooms neat. I go in there for inspection once in a while whether they are there or not. I know it isn't good form to go through dresser drawers that don't belong to you, but all I do is glance to see that whatever is there is neat. If I find a messy drawer with every-thing stuffed in, I just grab it on both sides and pull the whole thing out on the floor, or dump it over on the bed. That's my subtle message to the chil-dren. They don't say anything when they get back, they just put it in order.

So far, I guess, I may sound pretty bossy and in-tolerant. I am working on that, because I don't admire that attitude very much. The trouble is that I am a very observant person, and it bothers me when things are out of order. When I was younger and less tempered, I used to speak more often about the things I observed. As I get older, however, I observe, but don't speak quite so much.

I have had some insight lately to show that it makes a great difference in me whether I am letting my head or my heart do the observing. When my head is in action, *you* are in trouble. When my heart rules things, which is now about two-thirds of the time, then *I* am more likely to be the one getting in trouble. That's no good; that I must work on.

In matters of housework or business or anything at all, you really cannot change another person fundamentally. I shall not try to make that change in another person, but there is another line that goes with that. Neither should the other person try to change me. I tried very hard to be a proper mixture of the oak and the willow. The oak is very strong, but if it won't bend at all, it must break. If the willow can move with every breeze and then stand up again, it can live forever. Mama always wanted me to stand as strong as the oak. It has been for me to learn that you have to bend also. Job 31, Verse 6 says "Let me be weighed in an even balance." I strive for balance in my mind. The balance of my emotions, the balance of eating and living and rest-ing—a balance of exercise and a balance of love.

I have found a way to eliminate some confusion, do a little teaching and make life easier on every-one in the family. I make up a little chart of re-sponsibilities each week and hang it on the kitchen wall. It shows what each person is supposed to do each day of the week. I am talking about myself and the children. Whatever you are doing in the theater, the office, or at home, you do need some routine to get things done, and it builds good habits. People always figure me to be an "ad-lib" person. There is some truth to that, but I am very routine about some things.

On Monday, our kitchen gets completely wiped down—everything, woodwork and all. I am a nut about woodwork wherever it is. I've seen some women who call themselves great housekeepers, but if you look at the baseboards around the floor, you find scuff marks and dirt there. That just doesn't add up to a great housekeeper as far as I'm concerned. Or look at window sills and shutters. Oh yes, it's hard to be a really good housekeeper. I think it's a joke when some women get on television and say, "I'm *just* a housewife." A good housewife is a woman of great art and skill. If she is doing a good job, she has a right to take a deep bow as much as any performer on the stage or television. The home is her castle. The king goes out and the queen sits within and takes care of things.

Incidentally, have you ever noticed that when another queen enters the house, it can create trouble? You are very lucky if you can live with just your husband and your children in the house. Two queens cannot sit on a throne together. If you have to have in-laws or long-term guests, try to set them apart.

When I first started with the charts, my children and the occasional housekeepers (I had to hire some while I was on the road) resented them pretty much. As time went along, they found out that it worked pretty well. We do a couple of rooms each day, or sometimes only one. Then there are the regular chores that have to be done, but have nothing to do with the chart. We spread those out through the week.

I remember my Mama was fond of oiling the floors. She put furniture oil in a bucket of warm water and wiped the floors. They would shine just beautifully. Sometimes if we had guests walk in the house, Mama might just grab a dust mop and wipe up the tracks behind them. Every day when I came home from school in Philadelphia, I'd have the white steps to do. Sweep 'em, scrub 'em, and put paper over 'em until they dried. After all, in her words, those steps were our front porch.

When I'm at home, I write "Mama's Chart" at the top of the weekly duty chart. When I have to be away and a housekeeper is going to be around, I change it to "Pearl's Chart." If one of them resents having me lay out the routine, I just tell them, "Look, when you are in your house, you can do it your *own* way. Now you're in *mine* and I like my chart followed." Of course, as soon as I step away, they insist on having it their own way after all, and that's when we start to get in trouble.

The chart simply describes the *least* housework that is going to get done on a given day. If I pass the piano on the way to take a shower and I notice that it is looking pretty dusty, then after the shower when I round up the towels for the wash, I may just detour by way of the piano and lay one of those babies up there and wipe off the top. After all, the towel is going into the washing machine anyhow. It's a matter of being observant and willing to take ten seconds to remedy a situation. Once a week I oil all the furniture, and in-between all I have to do is keep my eyes open.

The chart, the routine, the regular and expected ways of keeping up with things will save you. It will keep you from getting too tired, and in the process it will keep you from *resenting* your house. It's a tragic thing when you come to hate the place where you spend most of your time, just because it makes you exhausted. When I am cleaning, I really move. I don't fool around. By eleven o'clock in the morning, I'm through with everything. In the summer, I get out of there and do something I want to do. Fortunately, I have a swimming pool in the back-yard, so I can go out there and spend a couple of hours. I also practice my golf stroke, jump rope, and, my dears, I use the swing and seesaw. Even when I'm having my recreation time, I make every trip across the place count for something. If I find myself going out toward the freezer room, I'll make sure that I bring back what I need for the next meal. When I get out of the pool and want my suit to dry a little bit before I go in the house, I'll take that time to dig a little around the roses or do some pruning.

When I first get up in the morning, while bath-ing, I may notice that the glass shelves over the basin are looking bad. That means that I am going to do something about it. After I take my wonderful shower or maybe my little bird bath (where I wash as far as possible and then I'm sure to hit possible), I'll just reach up with the washcloth, rinse it out and wipe those shelves clean. I keep ammonia and pine oil right under the bathroom sink just for things like this. What I am talking about is the spur of the moment touch-up. It can make all the differ-ence in a room, as long as that room gets a general

housecleaning once a week, *every* week. Believe
me, if you follow this advice, you'll never really be
busy with your housecleaning and you will certainly
never get exhausted. There will be no day when you
walk twenty thousand miles as some women do
when they let everything go to pot and then try to
catch up all at one time.

I think it makes sense to have a regular washday
and a regular ironing day. I admit that I send a lot
of things out, but I haven't always done that. Even
now there are things that we do at home. Dee Dee
and I wash on Monday, and we do our ironing
together on Tuesday. We do not let ourselves get
too far behind on either one. If a woman says that
she has exhausted herself from ironing all day and
night, then you can bet that she let that wet stuff
pile up in the laundry room for too many weeks.

We have it pretty easy now, even when things
are at the worst. I remember the time when you
had those three big tubs. I know about them because
I have had my hands down in there. In the washtub
you had the washboard and all the suds. Then you
had the rinse and the bluing. If you wanted something starched, you had to cook the old-fashioned
starch on the stove. By the way, did you know that
some women almost can't stand to do their washing
at home, even if they have a machine? They'll run
down to the laundromat once in a while. I think
the reason is that they like to keep in touch with the
other girls. There's a certain amount of gossip that
can go on when all you have to do is throw the
clothes in the machine and push the button. I guess
girl talk has been a big part of washday for a long
time, ever since the people of Biblical days used to
take their clothing down to the river and beat it with
a rock. Me, I don't like girl talk very much. I like
to have my washing machine nearby so I can throw
the stuff in there and step into the kitchen and put
on a roast, and then sit down and do some reading
and handwork, or maybe just lie down on the floor
and get some real rest, before the machine comes
to the end.

The chart should have a little flexibility in it for

special circumstances. I know that when I got out of the hospital and was supposed to be reducing my activities, I made a few changes in the chart. I sat down with my one-finger typing and I changed the chart for a while. I gave some of my items to Dee Dee, and also took some of Tony's responsibilities and passed them around among the three nieces who were staying with us for the summer. Tony usually has to feed the dogs and empty the trash. Just the smaller trash cans, because Louis has to take out the bigger, heavier ones. It worked out fine. When they hit the floor in the morning all the little girls made their beds, and Tony made his. The nieces were really Dee Dee's guests, so I let her prepare breakfast for them all.

I made one thing clear to my son and daughter. I told them that they were not allowed to make a monster of me in my own house. I told them to enforce the house rules on their guests, and to leave me out of it. "Tell them all what I like and what I don't like in the way of house routine, and tell them it's up to *them* to carry out the plan." I wouldn't let all of them get in the kitchen at the same time, because I knew there would be confusion and embarrassment when dishes were broken. Did you ever notice that girls between twelve and sixteen move around very close together? If one of them moves to one side, the rest of them move the same way. They almost run up and down each other's backs, in fact. If you call the name of one of them all four will show up, or else you get nobody. Parents today probably do a little bit too much screaming at their children and their children's friends. I figure that wall chart saved me many, many screams during the course of their visit this summer. They were to get through with their work as fast as they could, and then, bang, get out to the swimming pool or to the backyard to play. I said, "You don't bug me and I won't bug you." I meant it.

As a general principle, I don't like to meddle with children too much, because I think it is unfair to them. It makes it a little bit hard for them to grow up. I don't go to my children's door and listen to them. I don't go peeping around to see what they are up to. I let them make use of their time together or in privacy. Parents bring a certain inhibition with them, and I think the children at a certain age need a lot of time without that kind of inhibition. I think that in the beginning this came as a shock to Louis, seeing that the kids didn't want to be with us all the time. When we would travel or when we were at home, it didn't matter—Louis felt that the kids ought to want to be around us, to sit and talk with us after all the work was done. They do that sometimes, but, of course, when they start to get a little bit grown-up, they want to be out by themselves talking their fannies off without inhibition. I'm a pretty tight and tough disciplinarian with children when they have something they are supposed to do. When they don't, I try to leave them pretty much alone. I'm better about that than Louis, I think, but he is beginning to come around. He's changing his love from a hovering kind of love into the kind that lets youngsters grow up. I'm going to do a lot more talking about children and growing up in the next chapter.

Anyway, as far as housework is concerned, Dee Dee and Tony and their cousins performed beautifully. It didn't take them long to realize that if they missed doing something right the first time, they were going to have to come right back and do it all over again. It was good for them, a kind of routine personal discipline. Kids used to get that at camp, but I'm not so sure they get it at camps any more.

Do you get the impression by now that I am interested in thoroughness when it comes to maintaining my house? That is the fact of the matter. When I clean, I am serious about it. For example, do you realize how dusty and dirty the cushions on the furniture can get? I grab me a whisk broom and get all those pillows off there and get that dust flying. A whisk broom is a piece of equipment that most housewives don't think too much about using. Believe me, it is very valuable. Once you get that dust off the cushions, then you can vacuum it up easily. Also, I find that a whisk broom can get some things off of there that a vacuum cleaner might miss. When I vacuum, I don't reach my arm down under there and go as far as I can, I grab a piece of furniture and move it, because I intend to vacuum properly underneath as well as around.

Speaking of moving things, I think that I can move into a house faster than anybody you've ever seen, because I have a theory: I take things in order. First, I clean the house, then I get the drapes up, then I put my carpets down and I walk around with little pieces of paper in my hand. I write the name of a piece of furniture on a piece of paper and I put the piece of paper on the floor. Before that furniture gets in there, I know exactly where every piece is going to go. Somehow, I just know exactly what is the right place for each stick of furniture we own.

Our living room really never gets dirty from use, but just from being there. The fact is, we don't use our living room very much. My family and guests alike come in through the kitchen. Some of you probably would not think about receiving guests through the kitchen door. When I was little, the living room was considered to be a very special place. On Sunday, we got dressed up and sat down in there. In my present house, in the course of eight years, I haven't sat down in my living room once. It sounds queer to say so, but I never had a cup of coffee in there. We're not really a prim-and-proper family. And prim and proper is the way I think about the living room. Our guests almost always sit down in the kitchen, and we just talk there. Next to the kitchen there is a little room I call the music room—a very tiny place. It just seems to belong in connection with the kitchen. I have a television set in there and a good radio. There's a comfortable chair, and when you sit there you can actually see into the living room. The living room is a kind of museum as far as I am concerned.

In the living room, I have a chair from the White

House which President Nixon gave me after I did
a performance for a special dinner he had there. It
is one of the few pieces of furniture ever given to
anyone from the White House collection. I pass by
that chair sometimes and I say, "Gee whizz, Pearl,
my goodness gracious, the President's chair is sitting
here, the very one the President used that night."

There is something else that I always have in the
house—tropical fish. I don't remember Mama ever
being without goldfish. For some reason or other, I
always have a tank of tropical fish in my house.
Right now my living room has a ninety-gallon tank
and two twenty-gallon tanks underneath it. I use
that stack of fish tanks almost as a room divider.
Behind it, I have a little library section with maybe
a thousand books in it. I have read almost every one
of them, by the way, but not in the living room. So
I have these fish. I don't know half of their names,
but I think what is important to me is the light in
the tank. I have a ritual about turning on that light
every night in the living room. Louis has asked me
a couple of times, "Honey, if you are not going to
be in there, why turn on the light? The fish don't
care." He is right, I guess. We are always running
around in wet bathing suits and slacks. California
is a very informal place, so even when we have
company, we are usually outdoors at a barbecue or
by the pool. I guess it comes down to my feeling
that that fish tank with its little light stands there as
a kind of beacon—a sort of welcome light to any
stranger who might appear. It's like a way of showing that there is life out in the living room and life
all through our house.

Yes, I want life all through my house. My wish
for the living things around me is that they be ade-
quately provided for in every way. I want for them
sufficient food and sufficient order in which to
enjoy their home. I want for them a kind of existence that breeds peace and security. Having fish
in a tank, I violate one of my rules about taking
animals away from their natural habitat. To make
up for it in a way, because I feel the need of them so

strongly, I fixed those aquariums up so that I doubt that even the fish can tell the difference. The feeling I have about my living companions extends to my dogs out back. One of the worst whippings I ever gave Tony had to do with those dogs. He was supposed to give them water once when I was away. I returned in 100° weather to find those dogs dry, with their tongues hanging out. My theory is that if those creatures have become dependent on me, then I must take that responsibility very seriously. A thirsty dog can only come to lie at your feet with his tongue hanging out. Those old fellows seem to understand the rules of the game. I will do anything for them, and in return they must learn to behave themselves. They do, too. I talk to those guys just like I talk to any person, and I think they get most of it. The trick is that they know I care. If I am walking through the yard and I go give one of them a pat, and find that he is a little scruffy, and not smelling too good, then just at that moment I go and get the spray powder and do him up real good. He knows.

When you look at it a certain way, housekeeping is for the benefit of all the life from corner to corner in a house. Keeping the house in respectable condition is a prime family activity. It is one way for each member of the family to demonstrate practical love for the others. With the right discipline and the right attitudes, housework can reinforce a mutual respect among family members. Far from a source of resentment and fatigue, *housework* becomes *houselife,* a framework of devotion at the center of things.

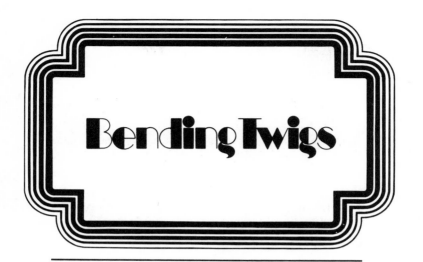

Bending Twigs

ONCE my children leave home, they may never cook a meal or lift a finger to do any housework, but they are going to *know how* it is done before I turn them loose. Furthermore, they are going to have a certain appreciation when they see those jobs done well by others. They are going to carry away from me a certain amount of know-how and some decent attitudes about the arts of running a house.

These attitudes must really begin in childhood. They have to be taught and nourished. I must do for my children what my Mama did for me. Whether they are rich or poor, married or single, I want my youngsters to give attention and respect to their home. I want them to be able to manage any aspect of a home, or help someone else to do it. A home atmosphere can be ruined by ignorance and reluctance on the part of the people who live there, or, if they know a little something, it can be a place of harmony, order, and comfort. One must be willing to give and one must know how to give effectively.

As I write this, Dee Dee, twelve, and Tony, eighteen, are both at home. I figure that I have pretty much done what I can do in the way of teaching. If the attitudes are not there now, life will do the rest. At the time that we volunteered our parenthood by adoption to each of these children as infants, we made a solemn commitment, Louis and

I, to give them the kind of upbringing that would give them a head start on happy homes of their own.

It takes a little extra time from mother to teach all the skills that are necessary. Then, once the skills are known, it takes alertness and patience to enforce the standards that you wish to apply. Children will, after all, find shortcuts, particularly when their interests are running in other directions. Nevertheless, it is necessary to instill in children the sense that a job should be done right every time, and that routine, systematic habits are necessary and worthwhile.

When I first got home from the hospital after heart trouble in 1972, I couldn't pull my load in the house. The kids had a chance for some real practice. You may be surprised to know that I require the same kinds of skills from Tony that I require from Dee Dee. I think every young man should know as much as possible about how to run a kitchen and how to attend to a house. Don't forget, they had a pretty rough standard to live up to, because I keep the kitchen in very fine shape myself when I am able. This experience gave me a chance to teach them something by giving them instructions from the bed. They didn't seem to mind too much, because they already knew that what they were learning was worth it.

Once I began to get up and out of bed a little bit, I could run an inspection now and then and point out a few things to the children. The first thing I noticed was that since they were doing all the dishes all the time, they had gotten a little careless. I found water spots on everything. It seems that they had resorted to an occasional wipe with a paper towel after the rinse; or else they were putting them in the rack and letting them sit there until they were dry. I can't go along with that. I like a nice soft dish towel and I like to see my dishes *polished* dry. I worked out an arrangement with them whereby if they did the dishes up to my standards for three or four days in a row, I would let them use the dishwasher the next day. I sometimes wonder why I have a dishwasher, because I usually find it doesn't do the kind of work I want done anyway. That arrangement seemed to please them very much.

Another thing I found was that despite all their previous training, they would finish up the kitchen, turn out the light and walk away without sweeping the floor. Whatever happened to sweeping the kitchen floor? To me it seems as important as any other part of the kitchen routine. You simply don't walk away from a dirty floor. That's an open invitation for bugs to come into the house, and besides, it just looks dirty. Now my Dee Dee knows that without any question after dinner one of her jobs is to take the tablecloth out and shake it and then sweep the floor. They know exactly how the kitchen is supposed to be kept, and, furthermore, they know that if I find it not done that way, I am going to wig out. That is something my children don't look forward to.

All this training and discipline are not just for the purpose of their later lives. It has an application right now. It gives me satisfaction and it gives my children confidence to know that they can walk into anyone's home, anywhere, and help out if they are asked. They will know exactly how things are done and they need feel no embarrassment or awkwardness. This kind of training, of course, has to go beyond the kitchen. But I think the kitchen is really where it starts.

You may already know this, but when you are trying to teach children, one of the largest things you have to do is to make them believe that they *can* learn what you have to offer them. Then you have to make them feel that it is *worthwhile* for them to learn what you are teaching. If you can get through these two steps, the chances are they will begin to perform, and the pride they take in that will keep them going from then on. The trick is getting the learner to the point of accomplishing something the first time. If a teacher is to succeed, he needs a learner. By that I mean a person who cares. A passive, uninterested student is no student at all, and that makes the teacher no teacher at all.

After Mama and Papa separated, Mama was living in Philadelphia and Papa was in Washington, D.C. I was the baby, so I was in Philadelphia with Mama. Eura and Virgie, my sisters, stayed in Washington most of the time to help take care of Papa. Virgie had a job and Eura kept the house and cooked for Papa. On my visits to Washington, I was learning from Eura, and she was also learning a few things about being punctual with meals. Sometimes she would be out in the street jumping "double-Dutch" jump rope—you know, with ropes going around both ways—and she would spy Papa coming up the street from work. With that cement dust on his face, he looked almost like a ghost to Eura when she realized she hadn't put the beans on. You see, it was Papa's habit to come home after a hard day's work, wash his face, and sit right down to dinner. Eura had to get that one straightened out. And Lord knows, she got straightened. Wow!

Papa could be a pretty rough disciplinarian with us. I don't mean that he was necessarily *physically* hard on us. I just mean that he created a tension sometimes that I think could have been a bit too much. You have to watch out for that with children. Normally, they care very much what their parents think of them. Some children need to feel a very close support from parents. If they feel that they are not getting enough of it, they can create an inside tension that can be bad for them, and their parents as well. I think that actually the mental condition of a child, or a grownup for that matter, can make him susceptible to illnesses. I suspect that this may have had something to do with the terrible problem Dee Dee had with asthma. She has always been a tiny little thing, and during her early years she had a terrible problem with asthmatic attacks. In the beginning, I didn't know what to do except ask God to help her. She began to fight the asthma and to do a pretty good job of bringing power to bear against it. At its worst, the thing was like a nightmare. During the night Louis and I were often up every fifteen minutes or so, up and down, up and down. Many times we had to get the doctor to our house at 2 A.M., or even run the little thing up to the hospital. We thought it might have something to do with certain foods, but that didn't turn out to be true.

Finally, when Dee Dee was about ten and a half, I said to Louis, "I'm so tired. She has tried all the medicines and she is dark in the eyes." Actually, Dee Dee was brilliant in school, but there was a listlessness from not being able to participate in certain activities. The child also was very thin. I decided that I was really going to work on that girl. I am not a medical person, but I know that the attitude of mind has a lot to do with the body. That summer I was touring with *Hello, Dolly!* I met with my sister-in-law from Chicago and arranged to have Candy, her eleven-year-old daughter, spend the summer with us. She and Dee Dee hit it off perfectly. I let those two little girls go absolutely insane having fun together. They could get through with their chores by around eleven o'clock in the morning and then head for the pool in the back-yard. I remember how much I used to love to swim when I was little, and there wasn't any pool nearby. I used to go to the public pool and pay twenty-five cents for a towel, or if I didn't have the quarter, I would try to find a swimming hole in the play-ground. They threw me out of every one of those places when I was tiny. I guess I must have been a nuisance.

Candy seemed to be great medicine for Dee Dee, who had never had any other girls her age nearby in the neighborhood. She had been lonely, among other things. Soon she was swimming freely in the pool and I remembered the times when she couldn't even be put into a tub to be bathed because it might bring on an attack. Asthma can really be something. The combination of happiness, exercise, and plenty of good food started to produce results. Today, Dee Dee does practically anything she wants in the way of activity and exercise. She eats like a horse, and in the last few years she has had, at the most, a dozen attacks. None of them has been as rough as she had before. She is pleasingly plump, a beautiful figure.

How did this wonderful change take place? I don't know, because I'm really no expert on such matters. I only know that I have seen it happen. The main thing you have to do with a disease or any other trouble is to firmly trust your Maker, knowing that He is the healer of all. The next thing you have to do, and it is related to the first, is to find a way to release your tensions. Don't take them on in the first place if you can help it, but if you must take them on, release them so quickly that you can't even remember having had them. It sounds hard, but it is absolutely not hard at all. You have to learn to let things run off your back like water off a duck. I know that this can be a little difficult, because through the years I have occasionally found a few drops sneaking between the feathers, and that can be irritating. I have learned that when I find the drops coming through to the point of an irritation, I simply try not to go so often to the water, if you know what I mean.

A pig is not dirty, the mud makes him appear so. There's another thing to notice—the pig goes to mud, the mud does not go to the pig. Sometimes it is like that with disease. A person can go to the disease rather than the disease coming to him. I think that with Dee Dee we may have given so much medical attention to her illness that she began to believe in it too much. She may have been going to the asthma just a bit, rather than having it actually attack her. I started allowing her to go on without the medicine for just as long as she could. Naturally, I wasn't going to endanger her life, but I just quit talking about it so much. Occasionally, when she would pick up something to eat that I knew had made her sick before, I would just ignore it. Another thing I did was to start trying to get her relaxed when she came home from school. Every day for quite a while I required her to just sit down in a tub of warm water and soak there for a little while until she felt rested. I could hear her in there singing and relaxing. Relaxation has a great healing force.

I'm famous for my offbeat ways of relaxing. That's why if I am cooking and I feel tense and weary, I'll just lie flat down on the floor. Flat out. I believe that any person who can be relatively relaxed and positive in outlook can arm himself against physical illness.

To Dee Dee

Demon
Delightful
Doubting
Happy
Daughter of Mine.

Hard Head
Handsome
Daughter of Mine

Loving
Laughable
Loud
Daughter of Mine,
  I love you.
    Mama, 1963

Tony is a fantastic inventor of sandwiches, and when I analyze his creations I realize they are quite good for him. One of his great big favorites is a sandwich made of *peanut butter, raisins, and bacon.* Yes! Another is simply *sliced avocado on bread.* There must be something there that the boy needs, and of course most teen-age boys do a pretty good job of eating. In fact, I think you have to see it to believe it! Here's a recipe that is a smash success with children.

FRIED CORN CAKES

When I was young I stayed in a rooming house with an old lady who passed this recipe along to me. She was Edwina, whom I mentioned in *The Raw*

Pearl. The cakes are very simple. You start with corn-meal mix of the kind that is prepared ahead of time for making corn bread. Add a little sugar and some eggs and mix it into a batter. Drop onto the griddle or the skillet the same as you would pancakes, and cook in the same way, turning them once (in butter).

In a way, I feel that these things are a nice change from pancakes. Children, particularly, get enough pancakes in the pancake houses on the road. That's especially true of my children, who travel with me quite a bit. The main attraction there is, of course, the syrup and butter. I guess there's nothing that children like to eat more than they like syrup and butter. Mine are particularly fond of boysenberry syrup; they cover everything on the plate with it, and sometimes cover the plate itself. I know when I put sweet potatoes on the plate, the children immediately reach for the butter. I tell them, "Wait, I cook with a lot of butter, why not have a taste of the real potato?" Louis just laughs and says, "Come on, Honey, let them have a little butter." He kids me about being willing to go out and spend money on clothes and trade in the car once in a while, and then I begrudge the children a pat of butter. That's not the point, of course, and we all know it. I just want them to taste the natural potato *once*. I want them to know how to enjoy life with or without embellishments. We are back to simplicity.

It's easy sometimes to forget that little children can be very thoughtful and sensitive people. Once you recognize the depth that is there, you have to deal with them in a new way. I remember one time in particular when Dee Dee was very, very small. She came into the kitchen and began to stir an imaginary pie. She seemed quiet, all of four years old. She said, "There's a lot of things people don't remember." I looked up from my kitchen chair and just stared at her. After a pause she said, "It's not easy not to remember. I wish it were easy for people to remember instead." I thought, "Yes, I guess I have felt the same thing and I am not a baby. Lord knows I'm not." She was still busying herself around the kitchen with her fantasy project. She said, "I wish Jesus could be here." That one stopped me. I had to drop everything and talk with her. "Why?" She answered, "Because he is nice." I said, "What do you want people to remember, those who forget so easily?" She thought about that one for quite a while and then she said, "I don't know, I guess I want them to remember the things that they need to remember." With that, and quite abruptly, she sauntered out of the kitchen leaving me and her imaginary cook pot behind.

I have said that children ought to be allowed in certain circumstances to choose what they want to eat because I think that often they will choose what they need. On the other hand, you can't be completely permissive about that. I think it is time for me to have a few things to say about picky eaters and how to help them in defining what's good. You probably know as well as I do that children go on appearances. They can take one look at something and decide that it doesn't look like something they want to eat. That goes even if they have never tasted it at all. I'm talking about things like broccoli and spinach. Even grownups on occasion will sit down at a table and refuse to eat something. No medical reason, it's just they never learned to like it, or even to tolerate it. On the occasions when my children take that approach, I ask, "Have you ever tried it?" They say something like, "Yes, but I really didn't like it at all. I think I must be allergic." I say, *"Where* did you try it?" Often they say that they tried it when they were smaller. I have been known to say, "Well, I would like you to do me a favor. Try it *now.* Maybe you have changed. Maybe you'd be doing yourself a favor too, you never know." I have had some real practical experience in converting picky eaters into enthusiastic eaters. The recipes in this book for spinach and broccoli are good cases. A number of children have learned to like these dishes because of the way they were prepared.

I really don't like to get a child at my table who

says, "My mother never made me eat stewed tomatoes," or whatever we might be having. I convince them to give it a try and then I thank them for having gone along with me on that. Usually, they decide that they liked it after all. I have been known to turn up my nose too, but when I do it, it is usually in a restaurant where the dishes don't look clean, or else the food looks like it has been left over. I would never do that in the home of a friend or in any private place where I was considered to be a guest. That's because of Mama's training. I think that now there are very few foods that I cannot eat with enjoyment. Even those things that I am usually not fond of deserve a new try every time they are served. I am always thinking that perhaps this cook will know something that none of the others did.

When I was growing up, my older sister Virgie was married to a gentleman who came from a large family, very nice people. One summer they went down to visit his folks and I went along to baby-sit. My fee, by the way, was $1.50 per week. I sat for four babies. When this big family sat down to eat, being about ten strong, each one ate something different. It seemed to me there were vegetarians and meat eaters. Some liked canned tomatoes and others liked them fresh. The interesting thing is that each one was allowed to have his own dish. That fascinated me, because I had never seen it work that way. Come to think of it, that must be the reason I decided to reject some of Mama's food when I got back. I figured if those folks could do it, I could do it myself.

Mama had a way of handling picky eaters at the table. Many are the times I have heard her say, "Give me credit for loving and caring enough to remember what is good for you and what is not good for you. For those I love, and I truly love you all, I'm not too much of a mistake maker on those issues." I remember one time Mama spread the table and I pointed to something and said I didn't really care for that. Mama had an expression, "No tea for the fever." I don't know yet exactly what she meant by it, but I got the general impression that it meant that she wasn't going to take any stuff from me.

Nobody in our family would declare that he wasn't going to eat something that Mama had cooked. Mama would say, "Young lady, are you hungry?" I'd say, "Yes, ma'am." Mama would say, "Well, everything is on this table that is *going* on here, and since you're hungry you can just eat bread. It's quite filling. Start eating now and eat until I say stop." Well, I thought that was just dandy, so I started eating bread. After I'd had a few pieces of bread I thought she would feel sorry for me and let me eat what she had served in the first place. My darlings, by the third slice my Mama hadn't even looked up to interrupt her meal, nor had anyone else at the table. So I just kept eating bread. Finally little Pearlie said, "Mama, I think I've had enough bread." She came back with a soft, "I'll decide that issue." When Mama finally reached her decision, your author was as well stuffed as any turkey on Thanksgiving Day. As Mama was clearing the table she gave her speech to me and all the clan. Her final words on that subject. "When you sit at this table, you will eat what I'm able to provide, without question. If there is nothing here to suit your appetite then you can eat bread or oatmeal. There's plenty of both. When you're older and can provide for yourselves, then you can pick and choose as you like."

By the way, when I was a child we didn't have hamburgers and Cokes and goodies in between meals. We'd have our breakfast before we went to school. At lunchtime we ate whatever we had taken to school with us. We came home and we had our dinner, and there wasn't much of anything in-between. I think that made it much easier for Mama to have her way at the table. She knew that she was putting wholesome food, well prepared, out there in front of us. She was right in thinking that if we were hungry we were going to appreciate that food.

I think that nowadays kids have a bit too much fun eating between meals. It's only natural that sometimes they'll sit down to the table without any appetite. That's when you start to get that real balking at the food you've prepared. Children are naturally hungry when they come home from school. That's the most dangerous time of all, because they're going to try to step over to that icebox and get a little nibble. They don't really know how to stop unless you help them. I help a little by planning to have dinner early. That means when the kids come home they know it can't be very long before they sit down at the table. If for any reason I know that dinner is going to be a little later than usual I let them have a piece of fruit, or a piece of bread with peanut butter, or a few raisins. They get just enough to make them comfortable until we can sit down to the table. If you do have a really early dinner at your house, you'll find that the kids also get hungry again before bed sometimes. Then a late snack is in order.

When Louis and I had the big kitchen at the ranch, I put two picnic tables in there and put all the food in the middle. Nowadays, I don't even give them that much choice. I generally serve plates from the stove, because we have a smaller kitchen. I put the food in front of them and say, "Dig in, and if there's nothing on here that you dig then shame on you." Brothers and sisters, if you get hungry enough you'll eat a lot of things, and come to like them. Just ask the *cannibals* about that!

I should say that there is one point where I draw the line on making kids eat things that they don't like. Naturally, there are some things that children react to in a physical way. If a child has a *physical* aversion for something, I never make him taste it any more until he wants to. It's amazing to me the way kids can put away junk without seeming to get sick. And yet they can take a couple of bites of something like good cheese, in the case of my Tony, and get sick at their stomachs.

I don't rule out junk food altogether, because I think it probably has a place in the lives of children. My kids get to eat junk on special occasions only, where junk is part of the deal. If they go to a recreational park or a carnival or to a ball game, they know and I know that they're going to get to eat some junk. Hamburgers, hot dogs, and soda. For them it's a special treat and I recognize that. I may try to remind them gently that when they get home we're going to have a full dinner. Sometimes I think they ease up a little on the junk when they realize that I'm going to be cooking when they get back. I also remind them that I don't want them to skip dinner and then come crying to me two and a half hours later about being hungry. If we happen to be at Disneyland or someplace like that when it comes time to have a meal, sometimes I'll simply declare that it is a junk day and they can make their meals the way they want them.

What about the babies? I must say that I'm not sold on canned baby food. I can remember the time when you could take some bean juice, some bread, and maybe some vegetables, and make a nice mashed-up business in a bowl and put that down in front of the baby. They would just gurgle ridiculously with joy. Nowadays people don't really think of doing that with a baby. Today it has to be strained this and that. And it seems to me that they've got that stuff down to the point where it all looks just alike. I imagine that if I had the nerve to *taste* some different kinds of it I would find it pretty uninteresting in that department too. Now that ought to get the baby food manufacturers down on my back. Maybe, after all, those foods taste better to babies.

It's very easy to prepare fruit for babies. You just chop it up and make sure that there are no seeds left in it. Actually, I suppose it's the same thing you get in those little jars, but somehow it seems more wholesome if they start with a regular piece of fresh fruit. Fruit is a wonderful thing to have around the house. I'll bet there are a couple of kinds of fruit that you've never thought of using for between-meal snacks. It's great for the kids and great for you. How about coconut, for example? You don't have to go to Hawaii to get one. You can pick them up often in the supermarket. I pick them up whenever they look good to me. I just take them home, poke a hole in there, and pour the juice out and drink it or share it with the kids. It's good for you. Then I crack that baby open and separate the meat from the hulls. Then I chop the meat up into little pieces and put it in a container in the icebox. If the kids really want a little snack after school, I let them reach in there and get them a small piece of coconut. They're delighted with it. For me, it's also a laxative.

Another nice little snack item that we use a lot around our house is cantaloupe. If you can get a cantaloupe that is ripe for eating, cut it into thick wedges and store it in a jar in the refrigerator. Let it stay cold and it'll be good for days. When you want a snack, you just bring out one of those wedges and enjoy it. Raw celery and carrots make good snack material too. I find that a lot of youngsters really like to gnaw on a raw carrot. I think children would like it even if Bugs Bunny had never existed.

Now I am about to give you a recipe that is wonderful from every point of view. For one thing, it is a terrific cake. For another, it makes oatmeal seem delicious to everybody, including the kids. I'm talking about the one and only greatest oatmeal cake in the world.

OATMEAL CAKE
(Mom and Pop Frank)

Mom and Pop Frank are people I have never met, but I feel I know them well and love them both. They sent me a fan letter long ago, and our correspondence began. They live in the country amid walnut trees, which provide them some activity and a little income as these two lovely people spend days gathering those walnuts and filling orders. Recently, I asked Mom Frank for a recipe. She sent the recipe for her oatmeal cake, and it is a solid smash success in our house.

The ingredients are 1¼ cups boiling water, 1

cup of quick oatmeal, 1 stick of margarine, 1 cup of brown sugar, 1 cup of white sugar, 1 teaspoon of vanilla, 2 eggs, 1⅓ cups of flour, 1 teaspoon of baking soda, and 1 teaspoon of salt.

Boil the water and pour it over the oats. Let it stand for about 20 minutes. Note carefully that you must not drain the water from the oats. In the same container blend the margarine and sugar with the oats. Add the eggs and vanilla, beat well, add your dry ingredients, and mix until smooth. Pour into a baking pan about 9″ by 12″ and bake at 350° for 35 or 40 minutes.

Now for the topping. I like that way of naming what you put on top of a cake. Topping. It sounds nice. The ingredients are 2 tablespoons of melted margarine, ¼ cup of evaporated milk, ½ cup of brown sugar, 1 teaspoon of vanilla, 1½ cups of chopped walnuts. Mix all the ingredients together and apply them to the cake while the cake is hot. That part is important. Then place the cake under a broiler until it is golden brown. That one makes my mouth water just thinking about it. You try it and watch your children eat oatmeal.

If a child generally is not a very good eater I think you can make matters worse if you insist on absolutely prim-and-proper table manners too early. The younger a child is, the worse it can be, because you know they tend to favor their fingers over their forks. I enjoy eating with my fingers myself once in a while. And you know there are foods that just seem to call for it. My friend Marie Bryant is fond of cooking foods from India. The kind that you properly eat with your fingers if you know what you're doing. Marie married a wonderful man from India the day after Louis and I were married. Actually Louis and I were the best man and lady for her and John. When she eats with her fingers in that style, she makes a beautiful art of it.

Just the same, I let my children know that I want them to understand the difference between eating with utensils and fingers. I tell them that I know that fingers were invented long before knives and forks, and that they are very handy for sure. There's nothing wrong with it, really, when you're out on a picnic. We drive across the country sometimes and cook outdoors along the way. Sometimes we're lucky if we have one spoon between the lot of us. Under those circumstances if you want to lick the plate, even that's fine with me. Great! What I object to is the kind of eating that makes any person look like an absolute glutton. That comes when he puts his face right down close to the plate and brings the food up with his fingers like some kind of an animal. You've seen people eat like it was going out of style, or like the Russians would be here tomorrow. My *dogs* dig into food that way.

Carol Channing is another woman who can eat beautifully with her fingers. She is very faithful about staying on her organic food diet, and that means she has to carry food with her wherever she goes. I had never seen deer meat until I saw Carol eat it with her fingers right off the bone. It was beautiful, because she knows how to do it. Of course, Carol also knows how to do a beautiful job with a knife and fork, and that's my point.

I do the same sort of thing with my children where clothes are concerned. I bought Tony a tuxedo two years before he had any real occasion to wear it. Of course, by that time it didn't fit. Anyway, Louis and I were going to a special place and taking Tony with us. The invitation said a tux would be in order. I made a pitch for Tony to put on a tuxedo, and I met with resistance immediately. Louis came to Tony's defense and said, "Gee, Honey, you know everybody's not going to have on a tux." I said, "Louis, how do you know everybody's *not* going to have on one? I spent the money two years ago, and I have never seen my check on his back."

Now I can tell you what you probably already know. I didn't care whether everybody was going to have on a tux or not. I just wanted to see my Tony, big and tall, all dressed up like a man. I was proud of him and I wanted him to see himself that way too. It's all right with me how he chooses to dress most of the time. But while he is doing that I want

him to know the difference. I want him to know
that there is a choice. A good alternative. We got
him all suited up for one night anyway, and it was
worth it as far as I'm concerned.

While we are talking about children, growing
up, manners, and all the rest, I'd like to put in a
good word for the Scouts. The Scouting organization
can be good for a youngster even when he doesn't
know it. Tony was a good case in point. I wanted
Tony to be a Boy Scout so badly in 1963 that I
decided to become a Den Mother myself. And you
know that means I wanted it pretty badly! Those
eight little creatures of God came trooping through
my gate and I found them to be both exasperating
and inspirational. Actually, Tony did not take to
the Scouts. He seemed more reluctant than the
others, maybe just because I was the Den Mother.
At the time, and for a little while, it seemed like a
terrible hurt. I had some selfish thoughts about it.
Wasn't I making a sacrifice? Why should my son
disappoint me this way? The truth of the matter is
that Tony is not a joiner and never has been. I
didn't exactly understand that at the time. He
wasn't rude or mean about wanting to be out of the
Scouts. I kept him in there long enough so that he
could see exactly what Scouting was, and I think
that even that little bit of the Boy Scouts did the
young man some real good.

I got enough encouragement out of that so I
decided to have Sister (that's what I call Dee Dee)
go into the Brownies. I had visions of Dee Dee as
hostess to a dozen little girls in our house. In my
mind's eye I could see them gathering around in
the kitchen while Dee Dee showed them some of
the cooking skills I had taught her by that time.
You know, those things never work out exactly the
way we adults imagine they will. Maybe that's okay.
Dee Dee made her *own* uses of that experience. In
her way, she is as independent as Tony is. Even
today, years later, I can look at that young lady and
see a flash of poise and grace that may well have
had its beginning there in the Brownies.

My children do know good manners, and they

use them most of the time, too. For example, they have been taught not to interrupt grownups in conversation anywhere at any time. Certainly, I'm not going to flap their wings and pretend they're little angels all the time, but they do impress people with the way they behave themselves around adults. Years ago, Carlton Alsop summed it up for me perfectly. We were having a conversation in a restaurant. He made the simplest kind of statement about manners, and I have never forgotten it: "There is no excuse for bad manners." That seems obvious at first, but if you start thinking about it, it's really a meaningful statement. *No* excuse. When you're talking about children, you have to think that there's no excuse for parents who *allow* their children to use bad manners. Children, after all, have to be taught. Anyway, if my children do have to interrupt with a phone message or something important enough to justify the interruption, they begin with a polite "Excuse me." They also say that when they step on a freshly mopped floor, for example.

Another thing—my children will knock on the frame of a door that is open. They know that it just finishes me off for people to walk in my door, even if it is open, without knocking. You might say, "Well, if the door is open, and if you're just talking about walking into a room, what are you getting so excited about?" I just think it's impolite, that's all. My children used to say, "But the door was open." And I would answer, "But you never heard anyone say to come in." It goes back to my general theory about the house. The house is your castle and when you step across the threshold of someone's castle without his permission, you have to be ready for battle.

Children, our joy, come to us as gifts, the miraculous material from which truly human beings can be made. I can never forget the purity of the thrill Louis and I felt when we received Tony and Dee Dee. With the excitement came a powerful sense of responsibility, and all of you parents will know what I mean. Mothers and fathers want for their children a full measure of skill, peace, love, and satisfaction in living. These qualities come to young people through a kind of mystical recipe— parental example, challenge and support, freedom and discipline, and always the evidence that they are loved. We have to remember that while grow- ing up a child is a changing mixture of the person he *is* and the person we *hope* for him to be. We must love *both,* for if we push *too* hard we can be defeated by our own parental impatience, insecurity, and selfishness.

For the time they are with us, we arrange the ingredients of their lives as God and the instincts of good sense would dictate. We warm our children slowly, season them with discipline, baste them with affection, and trust in the outcome.

The Magic
of Mealtime

F PLANNING, shopping, and cooking are special acts of love, then surely mealtime is the ultimate ceremony, the ritual outcome of all this loving activity. Mealtimes in a family at home have importance that goes beyond the food. I have certain preferences about the way the mealtime is conducted, because I want this part of our lives to have as much significance as possible for all of us.

I have preferences about big things and preferences about little things. In this chapter, I'll mention some of each, and I'll ramble on a bit about how I look at the importance of mealtime and conduct at the table.

Just for openers, let me tell you that I don't put candles on my table at home. As far as I'm concerned, in my house candles are for the situation where the electricity blows out. I also keep a few kerosene lamps around for that situation. I do not want candlelight at my dinner table at home. One reason is that I don't particularly care to have my home bearing a resemblance to a restaurant. Good or bad. Restaurants are restaurants and home is home. In my dining area I want the lights up so that I can see everything that is going on and everything that is going into my mouth.

Now let me turn around and say that I don't have anything against candlelight in good restaurants. I say *good* restaurants because candlelight in

116

a bad restaurant can cover a multitude of sins. I guess I'm just naturally a little suspicious about the food that's put in front of me. I don't prefer roasted flies by candlelight. In a good restaurant though, one that has proved to me that it is clean and reliable, I like the intimacy that comes with candlelight.

To most people, intimacy in dining means that there is a closeness, a coziness, that surrounds the table. It means that to me too, but it also means that the place is dark enough so that people are not going to pay special attention to me because I'm a celebrity. I'm talking about the other guests at the restaurant. Intimacy means privacy to me as well as atmosphere.

When I first started getting stage jobs, the other girls and I would leave our pancake make-up and our theatrical mascara and everything on when we went out to eat after a show. They had something then called "beading," which we used to make up our eyes. Colgate made it, I think, and everyone in the theater used it. You warmed this black stuff and then with a brush or even a matchstick you kept applying it to your lashes until little beads appeared at the end of each lash. Then they were long and luxurious-looking. Oh, how I batted mine about! Now, of course, false eyelashes are for every woman, it seems. Here comes another industry down on my back, but I actually think that those false eyelashes can eventually pull out all of your own lashes. In the beginning everybody grabbed onto the idea and started wearing them when they didn't really need them. And finally they've become a necessity, because a lot of women just about don't have eyelashes any more, including yours truly.

Anyway, this beading was a lot of fun. You could go into the water and swim, and unless you put the little beads out on the end a lot of people couldn't tell that you had the stuff on. Of course, we wore brighter lipstick and heavier make-up in every respect. The funny thing is that we didn't want to go into dimly lit restaurants. In there, nobody could tell that we were from the theater. So at that time we used to like to go into a place that had pretty good light. In fact we loved all that light. It was almost like the stage. We would do a little prancing around there in the restaurant. People could just tell that we were theatrical. We enjoyed the glamor of that.

I also don't like *loud* restaurants, but then who does, really? In France and Italy, the restaurants are often quite noisy because over there they approve of a lot of chatter at the table. And sometimes, when they have to make themselves heard, that chatter can get pretty loud. In England, I guess it's a little different. Things are a bit quieter over there because they handle their knives and forks differently and they're pretty busy with that. They manage to move the food into their mouths pretty well too; stiff upper lip and all. If you've ever watched them push that food around and turn the fork over, they always look polite to me, but I get the distinct impression that they're always absolutely shoving it in. The British are generally very good about manners.

Speaking of manners, I had to pick some of my fancy table etiquette up along the way. Years ago, I found myself on the *Queen Mary* on the way to London. The first mealtime was a real shock. I never saw so much silverware in my life. It seemed to me it was on both sides of my plate, and up at the top of my plate, and everything looked pretty much alike. I didn't know where to begin. Until then I had been feeling pretty piss-ass elegant. Suddenly, I felt like an ignorant foreigner. There must have been ten or eleven utensils in front of me. For a flashing moment it occurred to me that maybe someone had forgotten to finish setting the table and had just left everything at this particular location.

There was nothing for me to do but become a good student. I watched carefully what other people did, and in what order, and then I followed suit. That's a little technique that I've taught my children. If they get themselves into a situation where they don't know about etiquette, they can learn quite a bit by watching. On a boat there are all kinds of people up and down the line to serve you in the dining room; that takes a little learning too —the waiter, the captain, the busboys, the stewards of various kinds. They go up the line and down the line. By the time you get dessert, you've got a little boy about twelve years old bringing that. There's a great tradition of training. They get these boys when they're pretty young, and I think that is good, because by the time they are adults they have an accomplished way of doing something special. I don't know whether you have noticed it, but we have lost many of our training grounds in this country. Our educational system is not training people for a wide variety of trades. The idea seems to be that everybody *should* go to college, and everybody is *going* to. I really think that the old European tradition of putting a young boy under the supervision of a skilled man is a very good idea.

At my table at home we really don't encourage too much talking. The main business there is eating and enjoying a wonderful meal. Oh, we have *some* laughter and talk. We're not really the most silent group in the world sitting there at the table, but consistent or overbearing chatter really bothers our enjoyment of a meal. The worst thing, of course, is when sometimes an argument may develop between parents and children. There's no place for that at the table. It ruins a meal completely. An argument spoils the whole damn thing. When an argument begins at the table all stomachs start to turn; and when one is not relaxed one can't really enjoy a meal. My belief is that at the table we should leave everything alone except eating and happiness.

That means that when we do have chatter, we have happy chatter and we avoid subjects like politics, religion, and race. Louis is particularly strong for happy conversation at the table. I remember that at my table when I was a child I used to catch a lot of conversation from my parents. By that I mean that they used to pick that time to tell me what I'd been doing wrong. I think Louis's way is better. It's my way too, now, but it wasn't always.

I think that if the man of the house is not relaxed when he gets home he should take a few minutes to cool down before he starts to sit down for a meal. That may mean a martini, and one certainly will do it. It may mean that he goes out into the yard and walks around a bit and relaxes, or puts on some comfortable clothes. If he comes home tense and hits the table directly, the chances are good that he's going to have indigestion. He's setting himself up for Rolaids.

I cut off a lot of things when it comes to be dinnertime, like the radio. We're very much against having the television set on during meals. It's a complete distraction, and nobody even knows what he's eating. When my kids try to watch TV and eat at the same time, they practically miss their mouths with food. When the children were small, Louis and I used that time to listen to the news, but the news is such *bad* news most of the time these days that we don't allow that at the table any more. Music is much better for relaxation. Sometimes music can be a good way to close down a conversation that's taking a wrong turn. I just excuse myself, get up, and turn the music up louder. I can make it pretty hard to have a bad conversation at the table.

If anybody insists on ruining the meal that I have prepared, then I let him know about it. I don't care if it's a guest or a member of my family. I tell them, "You have ruined this meal; all of the taste has gone out of the food."

Telephones represent a real problem at mealtime. I don't know about your house, but our phone rings a lot. Louis has business, I have business, the kids have friends. It bugs me when somebody calls at mealtime. When that phone rings in the middle of a meal, unless it's an emergency, one should answer and ask whoever it is to call back later. I know people who take the phone off the hook at mealtime and avoid the situation entirely. I love to do that. I don't suppose the phone company would care too much for it though.

Children, especially small children, can make pretty much confusion at the table. When ours were small, Louis and I heard about some other couples who would feed the kids first, and then later, with the kids out of the way, they would enjoy a quiet, peaceful dinner. Louis and I decided to try that. I fed the kids and sent them on their way, and then later Louis and I would sit down and try to eat. It just wouldn't work out. Louis was accustomed to having everybody together at the table, and actually that's the way I had always known it in my home too. We sat there and fell to complete silence. We were eating and everything was peaceful all right, but there was absolutely zero conversation. The fact is that both of us were sitting there missing the children. The experiment didn't last too long in our home.

I think that children should start off eating at the table with their parents and their brothers and sisters from the very beginning. And they should stay there right up to the time that they leave home. By the time children are six or seven years old, I believe that they should know how to behave at the table. Mine had to learn that, because when they reached an age of responsibility, at about six, they found out that if they had trouble at the table I would take them *away* from the table and speak to them with the palm of my hand on that little bottom. Table manners are very important to me. And eating together brings a certain unity that you can't get in any other way.

I don't think it is good for families when the children are out running around and then come home and miss the mealtime, go to the refrigerator, and begin to try to take care of themselves. Your house becomes something like a hotel with people coming and going all the time. If there's no time to sit together in harmony at mealtime, then try to *make* time. Meals offer the best chance we have to be together regularly.

Maybe you're beginning to think that the Bellson household is pretty old-fashioned. That is correct. We are old-fashioned about our meals and about our family. For example, I've taught my children to say some kind of grace at every mealtime, whether they are at home or not. If they go into a restaurant or if they're eating on the train, they sometimes are tempted to plunge right into the food. I stop them right there and remind them that God is everywhere, even on the train, and they shouldn't be ashamed to say grace. I don't require that they say it loud or even that they say anything at all from their mouths. It doesn't matter to me whether they go with the big tone or not. I don't have to hear a thing. But if I see them pause for a moment and lower their eyes, I think it is good, because I know that they are saying thanks to God.

BEEF STEW
À LA TRAIN

If my schedule would allow it, I would always take the train, for long trips and short trips alike. I'm tense on airplanes, but I find that trains are more relaxing. The food is good too, sometimes especially good. I remember one particular trip on the Sante Fe Superchief. I ordered beef stew and it was just delicious. I told the waiter, and he must have passed the word along to the chef, who rushed out there on the double. Well, maybe it was on the single, because he was not exactly a teeny-weeny man. Two to one, he devoured quite a bit of his own cooking. We chatted a bit as he stood there bouncing back and forth in the aisle and I suggested that he share the recipe with me. I told him he ought to let a lot of those plane riders know what's going on down on the ground. A beef stew like his might invite a few people down from the sky. He sweetly obliged, and I'm pleased to pass this wonderful recipe to you.

For home quantities, the ingredients are: 2 pounds beef chuck, 4 tablespoons of tomato puree,

3 to 5 carrots, 1 to 2 onions, 2 to 4 potatoes, 2 to 4 stalks celery, pinch of garlic, 1 tablespoon onion salt, 4 tablespoons flour.

Flour and braise the beef until brown (large chunks). Put it into a pot and cover with beef stock made from the puree (or use consommé). Slice and sauté the onions, carrots, and celery.

Season and cook the beef slowly, covered, until about ¾ done (size of chunks will determine how long). Then add potatoes. About 15 minutes before the end, add vegetables.

What really turns me off, though, is to go to a restaurant where there will be a buffet or a smorgasbord with food piled right out to the edges. I know you've seen people go up to that table and heap their plates up with four or five meats and three or four vegetables. It is a waste, a kind of gluttony that nauseates me. They pay a flat price there and then when they go up everything looks like a free-bee to them. They're going to see how much food they can take for their money. Number one, they don't even know half the things they're putting on there, and number two, they know very well that they cannot possibly eat it all. I find it much nicer to put a few things on there, and then if you're still hungry after you've eaten that, most places will allow you to return to the smorgasbord. Anybody knows that when you take six or seven things on a plate and heap it up there, and add a few pickled beets, it isn't going to work. I have seen genuinely hungry people in the world. Thinking of them makes bad smorgasbord behavior even more shameful. These same people who pile up the plate typically let their children do exactly the same thing without any supervision. That food is wasted.

I think that some people believe that having a lot of food means that they are having an elegant meal. I find no correspondence between the amount of food and the elegance of the mealtime. When I have my way about things I prepare and serve a few things simply. I have enough for everyone, and usually a little left over. I serve at the table with what I hope is simplicity and grace. I draw the line on simplicity when it comes to paper plates and paper cups. There's no place for them in our house. Some people will, you know, use paper in order to save dishwashing or whatever. When I started in the theater traveling as a teen-ager through the coal circuit in Pennsylvania, I had it up to my neck with paper plates and paper cups. I traveled by bus and occasionally by train (coach), and when I worked a place I usually was allowed to have some food there. I'm talking about restaurants, cabarets, and bars in small mining towns. Often I would have to get my food on a paper plate, cover it with a napkin and take it out to eat it. Ever since that time a paper plate or a paper cup just seems to take the taste away from my food. It didn't in those days, of course, because I couldn't do any better. There's nothing wrong with paper plates on a picnic, but I still prefer real plates and real cups. When we're going on a picnic or traveling across country where we might want to stop and cook up a little something, I always have a big cardboard box in the trunk of the car. It has my big skillet and some regular plates and cups that I reserve for that purpose. I don't care whether we break these things or not. The point is that we have them and we avoid that paper business. Memories, memories.

POTATO SALAD

This is my favorite cold dish for picnics or any other occasion, and I'll bet it's simpler than any potato salad you ever heard of.

Enough for days and days: 5 pounds white potatoes boiled just so, 2 dozen eggs (yes!) hard-boiled, 4 onions, tons of mayonnaise, salt and pepper to taste.

All other ingredients are a waste of time. The secret is the eggs, so don't hold back.

TURKEY DRESSING
À GO GO

Telling you about the beef stew reminded me about another recipe I got on the train one time. It was around Thanksgiving time. I was traveling to New York with my sister-in-law, Dee Dee. In the diner we shared a table with a wonderfully dressed, dignified woman who enjoyed our conversation for a little while as we discussed turkey and the many ways that it could be prepared poorly—too dry, etc.

Suddenly this lady, our marvelous companion, said that she knew of a new way to prepare turkey with dressing. One that was delicious and easy. I expressed interest and she said, "Here, let me write it down for you." She had been in the club car playing gin rummy, and she just pulled her score card out of her purse and began to write the recipe on the back. Dee Dee and I continued to eat. After a few moments of very careful writing, the lady handed the card over to me and I began to read. "Two cups of bread crumbs, 1 cup of butter, 2 onions, 1 teaspoon of salt, 1 teaspoon of pepper, and celery salt to taste." Then there was one more ingredient, "1 cup of popcorn kernels. You prepare this dressing, stuff the turkey full and put it in the oven. Bake until the popcorn begins to pop and the turkey's ass flies across the room." I wonder if she still lives in Calumet City, Iowa.

I believe in having a definite time to begin a meal and I believe in ending it when people are through eating. That may sound obvious, but some people don't subscribe to that view. They hang on at the table like it was a life raft. When Louis and I were first married, we used to go to my in-laws' house, and they had a different tradition. Their tradition, it seemed to me, was that they *never* ended a meal. When I was growing up, each meal was separate. You ended it. And then there was some time in there, and then you had the next meal. These in-laws never seemed to clear the table completely. There was always some food on there. People would be sitting around the table even between meals. I like to get up from the table and clear everything off and do the dishes quick, before I lose my motive. If I don't get rolling with that real hot water right after a meal, I find it awfully hard to get down to the dishes at all.

In the beginning, I told my relatives that, no, I didn't want anything else after lunch. But they would leave cookies on the table anyway. Then, as often as not, I would wind up with a cup of coffee in my hand and sit down there at the table and start eating cookies, just like everyone else. Then it was time for the next meal and I really can't tell where one began and the other left off. That brought on a thing of constantly eating. Of course, in some countries that's traditional and quite proper.

Youngsters can get into that constant eating habit by running around from one house to the next. Everyone doesn't have meals at the same time, you know. I've had to teach my children a very strict rule. If they have already eaten at home and find themselves out somewhere else, they will refuse food, because they know that they have already had enough. They're polite about it, but they do say no. On the other hand, if they are *hungry* and they happen to be at a neighbor's house when mealtime comes, the neighbors are likely to offer them a little bit of something. Again they will refuse, explaining that their mother is at home cooking dinner and that she will expect them to come home with an appetite. Everyone understands. When children come home for dinner without an appetite because they've been eating someplace else, it not only spoils their dinner, but also spoils dinner for their parents. The reason is that the children will sit there and pick at their food, and rumble and make trouble and try to distract themselves. Also, they feel a little guilty. Until they are taught, children will automatically accept food without stopping to think whether they want it or not. Ours have been trained never to waste food. If they accept food, they must eat it. If they don't want it they should not accept it.

Do you begin to get a feeling about how important I think mealtimes are in the life of family? Mealtimes are the tick of the clock for a good family. Each swing of the pendulum brings all members of the family back to that central point. I love the days that I have at home, uncluttered by business —days when I can look forward to each mealtime with the ones I love the most. In the preparation, I find my meaning. And in the joy of mealtime, I find my rewards.

My fondest memories are days when everyone is home and I can go to the kitchen in the late afternoon and turn on my favorite soft-music station as I start dinner. Then, at the appointed time, each member of the family converges toward the table. With the light up high, the music down low, simple food and simple plates on the table, love and respect and tradition flow between people, even in silence.

I remember so many good nights like this when, having cleared the table and done the dishes, I called Louis and the children into the kitchen for a bedtime snack. At that time, we would cast our eyes toward the day to come and look back over the day that was ending. When the children were small, I would take them in to dress for bed, and turn on the same soft music in their room. Then, as surely and automatically as the pendulum retraces its steps, I would return to the kitchen to cook for tomorrow and tomorrow.

Guest Appearances

HE HOME is a private sanctuary, and mealtime in the home is basically a family kind of thing as far as I'm concerned. That means that I do not have a lot of dinner guests in my home. I certainly don't subscribe to the practice of using mealtime as a way of paying simple debts or fulfilling social obligations. Mealtime is too important to use for such superficial ends. When I have guests in my house for mealtime they are people who are dear and close to me and my family, and people who can enjoy mealtime with us in the way that we hold dear, a ritual of informality and love. I don't believe in putting on the dog for a guest either, because I don't have that kind of guest. No matter what the person's social or economic status, no matter what his position or power in the world outside my home, he gets precisely the same kind of treatment as everyone else in my home. I feel that every day I give my family the best that I have. I could scarcely do more for anyone else coming in from the outside.

I would like to explain some of my attitudes about having guests, and about being a guest in someone else's home. I have some fairly definite opinions based on my good and bad experiences of the past. Whether you are king or knave, queen or tart, a certain special kind of attitude and behavior are called for. Relaxation gets near the heart of it. For a hostess who has cooked for guests, there is often a tendency to think that if anything is wrong it would be the end of the world. That does not promote relaxation. Likewise, for a guest there is a feeling that he must be calculating in his behavior, and a kind of falseness creeps in. Everyone can sense that, and it can destroy the pleasure of having friends nearby. It takes a special kind of confidence and trust to behave naturally and yet politely. There is a personal confidence that comes from knowing that you are in the company of people who accept you completely for what you are, and require no falseness from you.

I got some confidence from show business. Early in my career, I used to worry quite a bit about whether the wardrobe trunk would arrive on time for an opening. I guess I had it in my mind that if I didn't have my stage clothes for a cabaret performance, I couldn't perform. Experience finally proved to me that it was not so. I finally had to go on once in the slacks I had been traveling in. The reception by the audience couldn't have been better. Now I know that if the macaroni and cheese doesn't turn out for some reason (and that seldom happens), we can make do with something else. If my guests and I are *enjoying each other's company,* it won't make a great deal of difference. I take reasonable precautions and then I accept the course of the evening as it may turn out.

Frankly, I like to have guests who feel that they can be physically comfortable, as they might be at home at mealtime. That means that if a man is too warm in his coat, I'd like him to feel perfectly free to take it off if the thought occurs to him. I take it as a kind of compliment if I find someone in the course of conversation just slipping off his left shoe because perhaps it hurts a little bit. Just think how many men have had evenings ruined for them because they have been strapped up in a tuxedo in some warm dining room. Generally speaking, I think banquets are pretty bad anyway, but certain kinds of clothing can make them even worse.

Of course, there is a line that you have to draw on your behavior in someone else's home. You can make yourself at home right up to a certain limit. I don't like for people to come into my house, as children are apt to do, and decide to use the phone, or open the refrigerator, or answer the door for me without asking permission. That shows a certain disrespect for the people in charge of the house. It is insulting, and good friends don't do that to one another.

When I'm a guest in someone else's home, I don't just automatically like everything that goes on there. Sometimes I have found people who lay it on a little heavy because they feel that I'm a celebrity and should have special treatment. That turns me off right away. It shows me that they don't consider me to be the kind of close friend that I want to be. Nevertheless, because I respect my host's right in his own home, I will never allow him to detect any disappointment on my part. My Mama had a saying that describes this well. She said, "If you've got your head in a lion's mouth, don't snatch it out. Ease it out instead." That means that when I find myself in an unpleasant social situation, I will go through with it, then ease out of the situation. I will not put my head *back* in the lion's mouth again. Every man's home is his castle. That is true, but I don't have to *go* there.

I suppose I'm more reluctant than the average hostess. That is because I use my house as a protection from the kind of strain that comes from being with people all the time in my work. If I were in different circumstances, I would have more friends over. Louis would tell you that on occasion I have sat in that backyard, or worked around the house for six weeks at a stretch without really going out at all. All these years I have been busy out there in the world beyond my walls. My reflex is always to give when people ask. That ranges from performances on the stage to the most casual conversation and autograph signing. When I am near people, even strangers, I cannot hold back anything.

Maybe that's why on occasion I have finally just dropped completely. When I'm in the house for an extended stay, that doesn't mean that I'm lying propped up in the bed recuperating from something. I recuperate in activity: making scarves, cooking, reading, writing, gardening—charging up my batteries so that I can give without killing myself when next I step outside. Under those circumstances, I do have people come to see me once in a while—maybe one person every couple of weeks. I prefer to be rather private, even lonely, in that house, never rushing, but always accomplishing something as my strength will allow. The longer I stay there, it seems, the stronger I get, the more coherent my mind and philosophy become. If I ever reach the point where I cannot give when I'm on the outside, then, of course, I am finished as a performer. These days, when I bring company into my home it is because the people I have chosen can nourish me and revitalize my enthusiasm for mankind in general, and I can return the same.

Anyway, one of the things I want to do here is to pass along some of the recipes that I have frequently used with guests because my family shows me that they were especially enjoyable. That means that these will be some of my favorite recipes, those dishes that I cook with real anticipation for my family and my friends.

BAKED HAM

Now you're probably asking yourself "What could be so mysterious about baking a ham?" Well, there isn't anything mysterious about it, but you and I both know that even a good ham can be botched up pretty badly in the oven. Sometimes the flavor just isn't there. It doesn't have that wonderful texture and sweetness that ham has at its best. I don't like precooked hams. I buy a good-sized raw ham and boil it. A 6-pound ham takes about 2 hours. Save the juice, by the way, and put it in the refrigerator, because it is wonderful to use in cooking other things. Then, when I bake the ham, just before it gets done, I coat the outside of the ham with sorghum molasses. The heavy dark molasses makes a coating which I then sprinkle with raisins. I wrap it up in foil and put it in the oven. If you want to open it up and brown it a bit, that's fine too. This is just a really good way to cook a ham. If you do it this way, you may just be tempted to eat the whole 6 pounds by yourself.

LOIN PORK

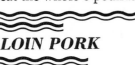

First of all, wash the pork loin. I don't know about you, but I sometimes think that I can't count on where that butcher's hand has been. Salt and pepper the loin and rub on a little flour. Garnish it with apples or pour in a little apple juice. Cook at 350°, 30 minutes per pound. When it's halfway from being done, add raisins, scallions, and garlic. Baste the meat often so the juice can simmer through the meat. Cut the outside so that the juice can go through to the center of the pork. I taste the gravy frequently during the cooking so that I will know whether there is enough seasoning there to penetrate properly into the meat. When the thing is done, if the juice isn't thick enough make it a little thicker with cornstarch, or the old fattening but beautiful way, with flour.

VEAL CHOPS AD LIB

I started out to prepare some veal one time for guests, and right away when I got into the recipe I found out that I didn't have most of the things it called for. It didn't bother me though, because that happens to me a lot. What I do in a case like that is to begin to improvise immediately. In this case, I'm sure that my creation turned out to be better than the original. I'm going to pass along to you not the recipe I started out to use, but the one I made up as I went along.

I whipped up some eggs, salt, and pepper in a flat bowl, and then in another flat bowl I got me some bread crumbs. This is one of the few times that I ever used bread crumbs to good advantage. I dipped the pieces of veal in the beaten eggs, then coated them with bread crumbs and laid them in the skillet. Then I got me a can of tomatoes. Most recipes would have called for tomato *paste* or tomato *juice* as mine did, but I didn't have those things on hand. The canned tomatoes turned out to be exactly the right answer. Anyway, I just poured the canned tomatoes and the juice right over the top of the veal and covered the whole thing with foil. Then I let it simmer for about 30 minutes. The outcome was wonderful!

While I'm telling you about good meat dishes to have when company comes, I'll tell you my favorite way to prepare lamb chops.

LAMB CHOPS SUMPIN ELSE

Mix garlic salt, pepper, flour (sprinkle a little on the chops), Worcestershire sauce, and bouillon cubes. Add a little water and pour the ingredients over the chops. It makes no difference whether you have the standing cut or the flat ones. Put the whole thing into a 350° oven, covered, for 35 minutes. Now sprinkle the top with the cheese of your choice and cook for another 10 minutes.

FRIED LAMB CHOPS
WITH A DIFFERENCE

Here's another beautiful and simple way to prepare lamb chops. I discovered it by accident. Once I had started out to fry chops in the regular way. While I was washing the meat I put most of a stick of butter in there for the 6 chops. I just put it right in the pan and started heating it up. Then I decided I might as well put the seasonings in there, so I put in the salt and pepper and Accent. It started to bubble and cook. I thought, Gee, I usually rub the chops with the spices before I start, but I've already got everything right there in the pan. I just rubbed those chops around in that hot pan and let the spices (parsley, onion, celery) and the butter brown the chops on the outside. Then I covered the pan and put it over a very low flame. That was it. The chops were most enjoyable and extremely well seasoned.

By the way, do you know what I like to serve with lamb? I like string beans and rice. It seems to be just the perfect combination, and I always get genuine compliments when I serve these three things together.

STEWED TOMATOES MICHELANGELO

These stewed tomatoes are so good that people have been known to stay over an extra night at my house just in order to help me finish up the roast pan full of tomatoes. They're actually so good that they make me think of a masterpiece like a Michelangelo! Of course, his masterpieces were of a different sort. These tomatoes are good as part of the main meal, or for dessert. It's your choice. You may think I'm building you up for something very hard to prepare. That's not the case. These things are as simple as they are delicious.

I generally make a whole big roast pan full and then I keep them around for days until we run out. It seems a shame to make just a few stewed tomatoes. I start with about 4 of the large cans of tomatoes. You may use as many as you like. Use about ¼ pound of butter, and sugar, salt, and pepper to taste. You'll find out after you've made these 2 or 3 times just about how sweet is perfect for your family. Now you're going to add old bread. By that I mean bread that's 3 or 4 days old and would ordinarily get thrown into the garbage or tossed out for the birds. You just break it into the mixture. The bread will soak up a lot of the juice and a lot of the sugar from the mixture. Once you have everything mixed up pretty well in the pan, put it in a 350° oven without a cover. Take it out when it starts to turn thick and you see a slight crust starting to form around the edges. Wowee!!

WHITE POTATOES
HOW DID YOU DO THIS

I think most people believe there isn't much you can do to improve the baking of a white potato. I have news for you all—when I put white potatoes on the table people take a bite and they are delighted and surprised. As often as not, they'll ask me the magic question. Well, here's how it's done. No big mystery to it at all. I make a little basket out of foil for each potato. After I've washed the potatoes and the oven is hot, I just pour a little bit of Italian dressing into that basket under the potato so that the potato is resting in it. As the cooking proceeds, the dressing goes all the way through the potato. You find the flavor delightfully mixed with the potato flavor. The skin of the potato is soft and edible. Try that one some time. If you prefer, you can use cooking oil with tiny garlic pieces in it. I keep a jar of that mixture handy at all times, even for salads. The longer it sits, the better it is.

CRISPY APPLE PUDDING

Here's one of my favorite dessert recipes. You know that I don't cook too many desserts, so this one has to be really good to get me so excited. I start with about 6 apples, peeled and sliced. Also, have on hand ½ cup of brown sugar, and ½ cup of white sugar, some flour, some lemon or vanilla extract, some cinnamon, and some water. Start by making a layer of apples. In one container mix the extract, the white sugar and some water. Then in another container blend some flour, brown sugar and about ½ stick of butter so that it gets nice and crumbly. On top of that layer of apples, sprinkle some of the first mixture and some of the crumbly mixture, sprinkle with cinnamon and a little more flour if you feel like it. The main thing is to give it some thickness. Now put on another layer of apples and repeat the process. When you have 4 or 5 layers, add a little more water so that everything is covered. I don't mean load the pan up with water— you just put enough in there so that it will be moist and won't burn. Cover and put it into a 350° oven for about 2 hours. At the end, brown the top by cooking the last 20 to 30 minutes uncovered. The result is a delicious crispy apple pudding.

You know, when we go to another man's country we are guests in something like the same way that we can be guests in a neighbor's house. Unfortunately, Americans are known throughout the world as complainers. That means that we are not really up on our best manners sometimes when it comes to traveling abroad. I had to pick up a few attitudes about that right after the war when I first went to England. It was an eye-opening experience for me, and I've never been the same about complaining. I don't do it myself in foreign countries, and I really can't stand to see another American do it either.

I went to England in 1948, my first trip. The English had not recovered from the war. We thought we had had it bad over here, but you should have been in England after the war was over. They had practically nothing that was any good to eat.

I was playing at the Palladium, and when I had time off I would go out into the street markets. I browsed and looked around for something good to buy, but there was nothing there really. They did have those little round baby tomatoes and big ripe black grapes. I remember distinctly going into a shop and buying a bag of grapes, which you could get without a coupon. My plan was to take them to my room and have them as my delicacy.

As soon as I paid for my grapes, I turned around and there was a little hungry face pressing his nose up against the glass of the store. I glanced at him with his nose all flattened out there against the glass, a child of maybe six or seven years. He had hunger written all over him. Well, of course, you know what happened. I never ate my big black grapes. I stepped right outside the store and handed him the whole bag. I just couldn't eat them.

People over there at that time were paying twenty cents for one egg, and that was when they didn't *have* twenty cents. In a week, they were allowed to buy maybe ten cents' worth of canned corned beef. They could slice that stuff so thin you could see through it. Families were lucky if they got two chops a week.

I tried to order chicken in a restaurant, because I figured that would be plentiful enough. Actually, the chicken didn't even smell good. I think that nothing over there was very fresh at that time. And when they served it, they served it with the black pin feathers still in it. Well, I started to object. I was beginning to think that it wasn't just that they didn't have enough food, but it was that they didn't know how to prepare anything. I still believe that the English are not really marvelous cooks. They brew a good cup of tea, but they go a little thin on the spices in everything they cook. They make a fairly decent trifle and good roast beef, but that's as far as it goes.

As cooks, the English just aren't in the same class with the French, or the Italians, or the Greeks. Still, I suppose each man cooks to satisfy himself, so who am I to talk? I started to turn up my nose at the food they were offering me over in England and then I stopped and thought about it for a moment. It just wasn't *right* for me to complain. I was a guest, after all. So I just added a little salt and I ate whatever they brought to me. These days things are turning around a bit. There are so many good restaurants opening in London that it's becoming rather an exciting place to eat.

To this day, it bothers me to eat out in European restaurants, because I know no matter how good the food may be, there will very often be loud voices complaining about one thing or another. It's the Americans. It happened even during that time I told you about after the war. There were Americans over there complaining to people who were barely existing. There were no green vegetables and nothing that was really delicious and nourishing. They had a few little round white potatoes and a few tiny tomatoes, and that was it.

The English make up for everything in courage. You talk about keeping a stiff upper lip—I can't imagine us over here in the United States keeping a stiff upper lip while going through what those people went through. When I was there, the windows were still barred up from being bombed and still everyone kept a stiff upper lip.

After I had been there for a while, someone really turned me on with a piece of news. One of my friends came to me and said, "Pearl, I know where we can go to get a steak!" Well, I couldn't *imagine* steak, but I was going to find out if there was any truth in it. It turned out that she had some kind of connections, and she *had* bought some steak, and she *was* having it prepared at a wonderful restaurant. I said, "Let's go, I don't care whether it's black market or whatever." Yipes! I started to get really excited.

We went into a very exclusive restaurant and I got my last few English pounds ready, because I could begin to taste that steak already. As we sat down, the big ritual began. The waiters started us off with a tall cold glass of lager, and I sipped that while waiting for my steak. Of course, while I was sitting there I began to think about all the most wonderful steaks, and they were getting longer and wider and thicker and more delicious in

my mind as time went on. Before very much time
had passed, the waiters rounded the corner. There
must have been ten of them, headed by a captain.
They were carrying our steak trays covered with
the bell-shaped tops. They put them down with a
great flourish and lifted those tops away, and
sweetheart, the steak was the size of one of our
sausage patties over here!

I looked down and I looked up at the English
faces beaming at me to see what pleasure I would
take in that wonderful piece of steak. For a split
second, I was in limbo, and then I beamed too. I
said, "This is *delicious.* What a wonderful *treat.*
Thank you so *very* much!" Finally they turned
their backs and went away. I took one bite and the
steak was gone. The fork almost disappeared too.

It was in London, of all places, during a *recent*
trip that I learned an important secret of good
Chinese food. Mr. Maio's Dumpling Inn, on Gerrard
Street, was the spot—superb food. As I ate, I was
wondering why Americans never seem to get quite
the right, full taste into Chinese food. The owner
took me to the kitchen and let me in on the answer.

BASIC CHINESE STOCK
PEKING (*Dumpling Inn*)

Peking cooking differs a bit from Cantonese, but
the stock is basic to all good Chinese cooking.

The secret is chicken bones! And neck bones—
only no meat. Cut the bones out of a chicken, or
several chickens, and boil them in a large pot of
water for 3 or 4 hours. I cook great quantities of
this to keep on hand.

When you begin to prepare *any* Chinese food,
pour some of this into the frying pan or pot. Then
cook the necessary meat or vegetables very hot and
fast. The Chinese can cook anything, even chicken
(in small pieces) in 15 minutes.

The 5 basic ingredients in Chinese cooking
are this stock, oil, onions, garlic, and soy sauce

(always last). By the way, they never thicken with
flour, but rather with cornstarch.

THREE-PART NOODLES
(Dumpling Inn)

Wash and cook egg noodles. Heat oil (extremely
hot) and throw in chopped raw pork, chicken (no
bones), and shrimp. Keep it moving, and fast.
When you're not actually moving it around, put a
top on. For the last 5 minutes, add drained, cooked
noodles and all the soy sauce you want. Eat till
you burst.

SOUP VARIATIONS
PEKING

Fill a pot with Chinese stock (see recipe). Bring
to a full boil and add chopped meat or fish (or
both). After 10 minutes add any and all vegetables
that you like. Don't forget about lettuce as a possibility, for it's good. Boil for 10 more minutes and
serve. Soy sauce may be added at the table.

CHICKEN AND ASPARAGUS
CHINESE

Heat oil until it's very hot. Add slivers or chunks of
chicken, keep turning, and fast. Cook for 15 minutes. Add asparagus and 1 cup of stock (see stock
recipe above), and cover for 10 more minutes.
Add soy sauce at the table.

SHRIMP
A GOOD WAY

Put raw or cooked shrimp into hot oil. Add as
much ketchup as you desire, and 2 to 3 teaspoons

sugar. Cover, and everything is beautiful in 10 minutes flat.

By the way, while the English themselves are not the greatest cooks, in my opinion (even when they have food), they just about make up for it in wonderful service. The restaurants have superbly trained help, beautiful attitudes, and a high degree of skill. There's no doubt about it. We can't do it over here the way they do it. So I say stop complaining so loudly when you're in someone else's home or someone else's country. Instead, we ought to just take what the people have to offer and quietly go on our way. After all, did you ever stop to think that when people come to the United States they have to adjust to us too?

In that vein, I remember a cute story from a young waitress, eighteen years old, in Canada. She had an American in her section one time who was making one unfair and irritating complaint after another. Finally, in a soft voice, the girl said to him, "Who was your twenty-third president in the United States?" He replied sharply, "I don't know," and then he started complaining about the food again. She said, "Well *I* know," and she told him. She went on to explain that she wanted to make a point with Americans who were complainers. She said, "We know a lot about you people because we are interested in you, but you never seem to bother to learn anything about us." That may be the key to everything, you know. If we would make it our business to try to learn a lot about the people and the customs, even the food, in the foreign countries we visit, we might find that learning something is more fun than complaining all the time.

Every place has its specialties. I think the French make the greatest sauces in the world. The taste of those wonderful mixtures is among some of my pleasantest memories of travel in that part of the world. The Germans really know what to do with a white potato. I suppose they must start off with the same potato we do, but that's where the similarity ends. They are great "plain-food cooks." They make it into a thing of beauty. Would you believe that the Italians make the greatest spaghetti in the world. I should certainly hope so. I'm offering Italian sauces in this book that can play in that league, though.

In the early fifties, Louis and I had a vacation in Europe. I had just closed, after sixteen weeks, a record-breaking stint at the Flamingo Hotel in Las Vegas. Louis and I were feeling so good that we decided to treat ourselves to a vacation. Of course, when we got to Europe we spent the first four days sleeping through everything, because we were so exhausted after being in the show all the time. Anyway, we *were* especially interested in spending some time in Italy, and we did travel around quite a bit. I had thirteen pieces of luggage; oh, I was really going to be the *grande Dame*. We rented a car and drove around. I had always heard that the Mediterranean Sea was blue, but I never knew that they meant it was blue like *that*. If you ever visit Portofino once you will have to go back. And then there was the food and wine. Even I liked to have myself a little glass of wine here and there in Italy.

I remember one scrumptious evening at the famous Alfredo's in Rome. The proprietor got out the solid gold utensils that he had made for Mary Pickford and Douglas Fairbanks, Sr. The violins were playing and the food was the kind of food that you never ever forget. We can be grateful for those special events that are so much fun to look back on.

ITALIAN SAUCE AS LOUIS LIKES IT

I start with a huge pot almost like they use in a hotel, because when I make Italian sauce I like to have a lot of it so that I can put it in little containers in the freezer. That way, I make sauce only 3 or 4 times a year. I start with quite a lot of oil, then add about 8 large cans of tomatoes. Now a lot of people use tomato paste or tomato sauce, but I don't think they make as good a sauce as straight canned tomatoes. Then I add whole, mild Italian sausages (about 20 or 30 to my huge pot), 6 or 8 onions, 4 to 6 cloves of garlic, mushrooms aplenty, and salt and pepper. I mix everything up over a high flame, and then turn to simmer and let the thing just cook down for about 3 hours. You want to stir it once in a while so it doesn't ever get too hot on the bottom. Season with great love.

Every woman who cooks with dedication and love likes to receive a compliment at the table now and then. As a matter of fact, I like to receive a compliment any time I can *get* one. It doesn't matter to me whether it is my family or guests from the outside who are sitting at my table. I really love to hear them say something good about the food.

I get my share of compliments too. The simplicity of my food seems to strike people. When I set the table and we all take our chairs, I watch as everyone picks up a fork. Then I just sort of sit back in my chair and watch for reactions. Every woman must do that when she has taken care to prepare a good meal. All I need to get me going is that one sincere compliment when someone says, "Hey, this is great!"

I'm sure that you've all seen dinners where the hostess finally had to ask. First of all that's a good sign she's worried about the dinner anyway. If you sit back for a beat and you still don't get the compliment, then I think you simply have to watch the progress of *conversation* at the table. If there is too much conversation, you can be sure that the food isn't as good as you wanted it to be. I find that when people are really absorbed by the flavor and the texture of the food, they are not talking a lot, and that suits me fine. I often feel that people who talk a lot at the table are talking to avoid the food, and hoping to finish without having to think about it too much. When it's quiet at the table, everyone is with it.

Now, although it isn't all about cooking, I'd like to say a few things about how to be a good house guest and how to be a good host or hostess for house guests. I've had a good deal of experience in this, especially with relatives.

I really believe that when a person is a guest in your house, it doesn't matter whether he is a relative or not. Take care of your responsibilities and don't expect to leave very much work for your guests. My problem has been made harder by the fact that I am a celebrity, and a lot of the people in my family think that they owe me some kind of special service, even when they are in *my house*. Actually, it works just the opposite. It gets me very upset to be treated like some kind of guest queen in my own house. I almost resent it when a relative says, "Oh, don't move, let me get up and get it." Or after dinner when they will say, "Now just let me wash up these dishes." No way is that going to happen. If there's some emergency reason why I have to ask my guests to do some work in my house, then I will *ask,* and without any embarrassment. Of course, there's another side to that too. When I go to someone else's home, I don't expect to be working all the time either. It really isn't my place to do so. If I'm asked to do some work in someone else's house, I will do so cheerfully. But I do not go around volunteering my services into areas which the hostess may hold dear to herself.

You see, when people come into my house and set me up on the stage and start working for me, it robs me of something very special. It takes away from me the opportunity to do for others in my love. There was a time when my relatives would not allow me to go get myself a drink of water out of the icebox, or dry a single dish. It practically drove me crazy.

I remember one time a relative came to my house and said, "Gee, I think I'll run the sweeper for you." I said, "Well, I think the rug is clean already." She said, "Oh, I know, but I just want to raise the nap on the rug." I started to get a little bit hard in my voice and I said, "Dear heart, the nap was raised when you *got* here." People must know by now that when I invite them over to my house for dinner, or for any afternoon, I have asked them there for one purpose only, and that is to enjoy themselves completely. I don't invite anyone over unless I am ready to make adequate preparations in cooking and cleaning. By the time they walk through that door, they must assume that everything that needs to be done has been done. After a few days of one particular visit from relatives Louis got up one morning and said, "Honey, I think I feel a little tension from you." Lord, he was right. He could have plucked me like a string.

I hate to invite a guest and then find out that I have a boss in my house. I call it "the great take-over." After two or three days of that, I come home with tickets to everything outside the house. I tell everybody, "Here's tickets to a great show and outside there's a pool. Everybody stop doing chores and enjoy yourself from now until the end of the visit. Don't lift a finger in my house." If somebody particularly loves cutting roses, I may let them do that and make a little arrangement, but I see that as recreation. I know that nobody loves the vacuum cleaner.

When I am a guest in someone else's house, I do the polite thing—I ask after dinner whether the hostess would like me to help with the dishes. If she says no, I let it drop right there and go sit in a quiet corner. If she says yes, then I'm up and busy until the dishes are out of the way. If it's an overnight stay, I think it's polite to make your bed in the morning. Sometimes a hostess will ask you not to. In that case, I simply obey. In short, as a guest in someone's home I do no more meddling around with household chores than I am asked to do.

MACARONI AND CHEESE IF I SAY SO MYSELF

Nobody ever has a little bit of my macaroni and cheese. Tony Bennett once ate so much of it at one meal he claimed he couldn't eat for a month afterward. Macaroni and cheese is my most famous personal recipe. I once tried to show how it was prepared on the Mike Douglas Show, and people screamed with laughter. That was because it had to be ready in about nine minutes of show time. I was really throwing it around. The prop man had taken my list of ingredients and had brought two or three times too much of everything. By the time I got everything rolling I was up to *you know where* in macaroni.

No matter how closely you follow my instructions, your macaroni and cheese will never taste exactly like mine, but we'll hope. I never made the dish exactly the same way twice, but each time it gets more divine. I've had people come back to me and say, "Pearl, I tried it, but it didn't taste like it did over at your house." I could have told them that before they went away. You see, no two cooks get exactly the same taste in a dish. I'm not saying that one is better or worse than the other. I'm just saying that each cook puts a certain amount of himself in there.

Now I guess I had better try to tell you how it's done. I prefer elbow macaroni to any other kind. When I start to make macaroni and cheese, I make the whole roast pan full, because macaroni and cheese is good day after day. I start with about 2 pounds of macaroni, boil it in the usual way until it is about ¾ done. Then I run cold water over it and wash away all the milky whiteness (starch) that will come off. In fact, I try to make sure I get every bit of it away from the macaroni. I even put my hands down there to separate the pieces so that the water touches every part of the macaroni. There's nothing worse, you know, than sticky macaroni.

Then I season the macaroni with salt, pepper, and butter. Usually 2 sticks of butter for this amount of macaroni. The next important thing to know is that you should use sharp Cheddar cheese, and pretty good cheese at that. The biggest mistake

that most people make in trying to prepare
macaroni and cheese is that they go a little short
on the cheese. I use *tons* of cheese in mine, enough
to go all the way through. After all, when the
thing is done I know that I'm going to call it
macaroni and cheese, and not macaroni and macaroni. Just chop it up into hunks so you can spread
it around generously.

Once I have the seasoned macaroni and the
cheese in my roast pan, I pour milk right up to the
top of the macaroni. By the way, when you're
salting the macaroni, keep in mind that cheese has
a certain saltiness in itself. So temper yourself. Next
I slide the whole thing in the oven at 350° (do
not cover), and cook it until I see the cheese starting
to melt. Then I take it out again and stir everything
up real good with a spoon. I want to make sure that
the melting cheese goes all the way through the
macaroni. This is important. At this point, I taste
it to see that the mixture is right. If anything is
missing, I put the finishing touches on right at this
moment. Then I shove it back in the oven (still no
cover) and let that baby just get bubbly brown
until I'm sure the cheese is fully melted all the way
to the bottom.

Now, of course, you can serve it hot. Then the
next day it's better, and the third day it's better still.
When it's cold, you can even slice it. That's good
too! When I'm going to reheat it, I just dip into
the roast pan, which I keep in the icebox, and get
out as much as I expect to use. Then I add a little
milk so that I preserve that wonderful softness, and
heat the whole thing up very slowly. I'm serious
when I say it's better the second day.

That's all there is to it, and there's nothing I
would rather put in front of guests than my
macaroni and cheese. I've even thought that of all
the things I prepare, it's probably the one that could
come closest to being a good commercial product.
The trouble is that I would have to be at that factory
all the time, tasting and tasting to make sure that
everything was just as it should be. I guess I had

better just stick to my kitchen and wish you the same success that I have had with this version of macaroni and cheese.

When you're in the company of good friends at your own table, there's a moment toward the end of the meal for sitting back and relishing the enjoyment of it. For me it comes when I'm mostly through eating, although I might want another little bite or two. At that particular moment, I don't want *anything* to interfere with the conversation and pleasure. That means particularly that I don't want anybody to get up and start clearing the table. I had a guest one time, again a relative, who felt that was the way to please me. She would get the jump on me by clearing the table and starting to do the dishes before I had even taken my last bite. I would say to her, "Look, Darlin', don't touch a thing. I'll take care of all that later. Just sit down. We'll have some coffee in a minute." Well, she wanted to insist, and there wasn't much I could do. I have Dee Dee trained. When I tell her to clear the plates, that's it, but she leaves the coffee cups until she gets the second nod. It's good to have that final cup.

Some people like to move into the next room for coffee after dinner. I prefer to finish it all up right there at the table. We're just a plain "down home" family. I've been rushed through many a meal in my travels around the country. I don't need that in our home. I really don't like to have outside help in my house, even when I'm having guests. They always tend to be a little too efficient about things. Another reason, I guess, is that they're just a little too much like waiters and waitresses, and I don't like that atmosphere in our home at all.

Setting and clearing the table really is our children's chore, even when we have company. I particularly enjoy having company when we can eat early enough for my children to be at the table. That wasn't possible, of course, when they were just little tykes. But now that they're older, they can take part in conversation and handle themselves

very well at the table. It only increases my pleasure.
They've known how to set the table since they were
very little, because I taught them a little verse, sort
of like a song. "The knife and spoon go together
and the fork stands alone. And what do you think
goes in the middle? The plate. The great big plate."

Anyway, when you get your stomach full and
everything is peaceful and happy, you want that
moment to pause. It's a part of my whole philosophy
of life. I live it with a certain rhythm, a downbeat
and a pause. The pause keeps it all together. I like
to sit back from the table for just a few minutes,
and then I like to have a big plain cup of coffee.

Speaking of that, it brings back wonderful and
amusing memories to me. My Mama used to sit
back that way and ask for a cup of coffee after a
meal, and I never thought much of it. But I noticed
something about her coffee drinking after I had
been away from home for a little while. Don't forget, I had made my start in show business, and
although it wasn't too fancy yet, I had been into a
few pretty good restaurants along the way. I had
learned that in the better restaurants they never
poured your coffee up to the top. The reason was,
of course, that they were apt to come back and give
you some more if you wanted it, and then you
would always have hot coffee in front of you. Well,
that wasn't my Mama's way. My Mama was raised
with a full cup of coffee, and that's the way she
meant to have it every time. Once on one of my
visits home Mama pushed back a little from the
table and asked for her cup of coffee. I poured her
one that came within about half an inch of the top
of her cup. Mama looked up at me with those little
eyes of hers and she said, "Honey, I said pour me a
cup of coffee." I said, "Well, you *do* have the coffee,
Mama. There it is. I've already poured it." Mama
said it again, and this time her eyes seemed to get
smaller. There was a certain firmness in her voice.
She said, "I want a cup of coffee, a *whole* cup of
coffee. Will you *pour me one?*" Then I made my
mistake. I pushed the issue even farther. I said, "But,

Mama, in the good restaurants, I mean, people don't do that. You're not supposed to pour your coffee all the way to the top." I went through the whole explanation with her. When she spoke this time her voice could have frozen the coffee pot and all the coffee in it. She measured out her words. "That's what they do out *there*. In *here,* you *pour* me a *cup* of *coffee.*"

Well, I don't suppose it would work out too well if I went around a table full of guests and poured everybody a cup of coffee right up to the brim. I do get a meaning from Mama's habit, though. In a way it's the same way I feel about having guests around my table at all. I start before they arrive, and I make sure that everything about our evening together will be filled to the brim. That's what delivers happiness to me, and it's what nourishes good friendships. When everything works out in an evening like that, it is a *glorious* thing. The food and laughter and unity of it all fill me to the point of running over.

A Little Help from My Friends

OR THE PEOPLE who make their bread and butter in the fantastic world of show business, regular home cooking and home living can be very hard to come by. It is in the nature of our business that we travel often, and work crazy hours when we are working. When you are starting out in our business, home life is out of the question. You have to be ready and willing to go anywhere to pick up a little job. You have to be willing to work any kind of hours in order to keep that job. Often there are no holidays, and in the beginning there isn't much money, either.

Surely it must be something else that keeps people striving for success in a business like that. The fact is that some people are "show business" by instinct. Performing is important enough to justify all the personal sacrifices involved in establishing a career. What I say is true not only of show-business personalities, but of most top professionals in general. Their schedules make it difficult for them to have what you might call a normal home life.

When performers and celebrities of all kinds reach a point where it is possible for them to arrange to have both the career and the home, it is a happy thing to see. These people can be more appreciative than other folks who have had their regular home lives all along. Folks imagine life on the road in show business (and the athletic world) to be one

151

glamorous experience after another. If you are any-where short of the top, or if you are not so flam-boyant in spending your money, it can be a fairly difficult existence.

Louis washes his underwear and socks in the bathroom sink in his hotel when on the road. Now it isn't really necessary for him to do that, he just does it by habit. It comes as second nature. I don't think there's a musician or a man in the theater who doesn't do some of his own washing when he's working a job. Some of them are careful to buy those shirts that can be washed out and hung up to dry; that way they don't have to send them out and pay the hotel laundry charges, which can be pretty high.

I get fed up with the popular stereotype about performers. People dream of us as boozers, dope peddlers, users, and everything of the sort. What they don't know is that we are very hard workers, and very few of us really get involved with any of those unhealthy things. Anybody, but *anybody,* who has worked his way up in show business knows what hardship means. For many of us, there were years of doing little benefits at prisons and schools, living in joints, and I do mean *joints,* and cooking in the bathroom on sterno stoves in order to have some-thing hot to eat. I have ironed on a towel on the floor of the hotel. I've ironed holding the clothes up against the wall, or even on the bed. In the years when I didn't have a dressing room, I dressed in a toilet with six people. Now, of course, because our business is a little crazy that way, I have a dressing room big enough for ten people. Anyway, I think that performers as a group deserve a little more respect than they get. In this country, we tend to put the big star way up on a pedestal, and everybody below that can sort of take care of himself. The English, for example, handle it a different way. They seem to have a universal respect even for the less famous performers. They also remember their performers longer. The performers themselves re-flect this respect, stars and unknowns alike. It's a wonderful thing to see Lord Olivier playing the butler, or Sir Ralph Richardson playing the cook, Sir John Gielgud as the porter. Those things really would finish off a lot of important American actors.

SMOKED HADDOCK WITH TOMATOES
(*Jane Churchill*)

A recent performing trip to London gave me a wonderful opportunity to renew my friendship with Jane Churchill and her wonderful husband, Lord Charles Churchill, brother of the Duke of Marlborough. At the end of one of my shows at Talk of the Town, I got both of them up on the stage to dance a little bit with me. "Bill Bailey," I think, was the number. Then the Churchills came backstage and we had a good visit.

I asked Jane for a favorite recipe and it arrived just in time to be included in the book.

Ingredients: 2 pounds smoked haddock fillet, ½ pint creamy milk, ¾ pound tomatoes, 1½ ounces of butter, salt and pepper.

Dip the tomatoes in a pan of boiling water for one minute. Then remove them and skin them. Chop them coarsely and cook gently for 4 to 5 minutes. Cut the fish into small pieces and place in a shallow fireproof dish. Over the fish pour the tomatoes, then the milk. Finally, season with salt and pepper and bake in a moderate oven for about 20 minutes. Serve with a dish of boiled rice and a green salad. It serves 4 people.

COLD YOGURT SOUP
(*Douglas Fairbanks, Jr.*)

When Douglas Fairbanks, Jr., walks into a room, everyone in that room can *feel* the man's presence. Maybe it is the bearing, the dignity, the smile, the obvious sincerity.

He and his lovely Virginia-born wife, Mary, live
in London now. Each time I go to England, I look
forward to seeing them. This recipe was accompanied by a note from Douglas. In it he said, "Pearl
dear, Here's the recipe that you asked for on the
telephone last night. Frankly, I know little or
nothing about cooking anything besides toast and
an egg! So this is really from Mary Lee."

Ingredients to serve 8 people: 5 cartons regular
size yogurt, 2 cupfuls ¼″ square diced cucumbers,
½ cup walnuts, chopped, or pine nuts (halved),
olive oil, a handful finely chopped fresh dill, if
available, or use dried dill (½ teaspoon), salt to
taste, white pepper, 3 cloves garlic.

Add 1 coffee spoon of olive oil to each carton
of yogurt. Stir in thoroughly and slowly. Add diced
cucumber, chopped walnuts, if available, or the pine
nuts, a handful of finely chopped fresh dill or the
dried dill. Add 3 crushed cloves garlic, salt to taste,
and white pepper. Chill thoroughly.

To serve, add 1 ice cube to each cup of soup.
This is most important, because it adds to the
consistency.

Banquets are a predictable part of show-business
life. I go to a good many benefits and things of that
sort. It doesn't make any difference whether you're
sitting on the dais or not, it's going to be beef and
mashed potatoes and green peas. Two to one, the
beef will get cold while people are making speeches.
Some people may not realize it, but most celebrities
have a bit to eat *before* they go to a thing like that.
You'll see them just sipping coffee during the whole
affair. They will tell you that they are not hungry.
A few years of that can make you appreciate every
single meal you have at home with your family.

I have told you about my trips to the market,
when I can fill six or seven baskets right up to the
top and spend maybe a couple of hundred dollars
on groceries. I don't do it very often, because I don't
have to, but when I do that it gives me a great deal
of pleasure. I like to come home and fill the freezer

with meat and vegetables and good things for me and my family to prepare later on. It makes me a little self-conscious when I'm moving all those groceries out of the supermarket, because I can imagine that people think, "Isn't that just like one of those show-business people!" I guess I just think it must look selfish and extravagant. What gets me is that they really don't know how *long* I'm going to be using that food.

It's like a show-business person to hoard up quite a bit of food when he has the means to do so. The usual thing is to find a space between jobs. Of course, for a star the job can pay pretty well, but you never know just how long it's going to be between the one you just finished and the one you're going to do next. I've had people look at me and I knew they were thinking I was some kind of big-time millionaire. The fact is that at the time, I didn't even have a job.

When I was first starting out in this business, Mama told me something that's been important to me. She said, "When you get a good job or two, pay your rent and get you some groceries. Buy things ahead and be prepared for the bad times if they come." That was Mama. I've told you about her and the sugar. She was for taking care of basic things first.

When I was little, Papa did all the shopping in our house. He too was a great one for getting basic commodities in advance. Once when I was very young that man went shopping and bought *one hundred pounds* of each *bean* he could think of. He stored them all up in bags and jars. I couldn't even tell you exactly why, I suppose it's a kind of superstition, but I do the same sort of thing today. In various closets around my house, like the one in my patio room, you can find dozens and dozens of big Mason jars full of beans, rice, spaghetti, and macaroni— the basic things.

I know quite a few people in show business who have reached a level in their careers where they can turn back to the luxuries of home cooking. Some are performers, and some are in the business side of entertainment. They are my friends, for they share with me, if nothing else, a love of cooking and sharing. I will tell you a few stories about these people and pass along to you some of their own favorite recipes, with their permission, of course. Also, I'll include recipes from some friends not directly involved in show business.

Think of it—his name has been a household word for many years. We know him as a wonderful father and husband, and we know his voice as the sound of "White Christmas." Who goes through any Yule season without hearing that song crooned by Bing Crosby? He is a man of many sides—a movie star who loves to fish. He is easy-going, and yet he is the hardest worker on any set where he appears. He is the first to arrive in the studio, even before some of the crew. Then when work is over, he is the last one to put that pipe in his mouth, slant his jaunty hat and saunter away. He is a man with a great sense of humor, and he is a dream of a human being.

I know of one time when I managed to keep Bing for quite a while after a taping.

The occasion was the first show in my series for ABC a couple of seasons ago. It was a wonderful show to do with Bing, Louis Armstrong, and Andy Williams. Our theater was the Hollywood Palace, which had a pretty good patio. I had arranged in advance to cook for all the crew and guests on the show. I sent some of my staff members out to rent tables and all the trimmings. Personally, I don't like to stand up and eat. Old folks used to say that if you did that the food would go right to your feet. Actually, I don't need anything to go to my feet because usually my feet are hurting too much for added attractions.·

I had done all my cooking on Thursday night after rehearsal—chicken, macaroni and cheese, and rice pudding. I had the staff bring in a bar and we had some kegs of beer there as well. I was prepared for seventy or eighty people, which is what we had.

Some of the things had to be warm, so I asked a friend to bring the food down in the evening. I had to be at the theater all afternoon. I wanted to be sure that everything was hot if it was *supposed* to be hot. I am a real bug about that. Fortunately we had beautiful weather, so the patio was perfect. We were prepared for the possibility that we might have to move into the balcony section of the theater, which had a place large enough for us all.

Bing sent for Katherine, his wife, who is one of the most wonderful women I ever met in my life. The office staff were all prepared to help out in the evening, starting around ten, for this fabulous dinner I had prepared. Actually, I had let them off from work about three so that they could get some rest and have a few hours off.

The whole thing was a fantastic success! Everyone had a wonderful time. No one made a move to leave there until between one and two in the morning.

I remember about one o'clock Bing was sitting there with his third dish of rice pudding, just shaking his head back and forth and saying how good it was. Katherine couldn't believe it, because Bing is usually so eager to get home after a show. That party was such a success that I decided to do the same thing every week. I got the thing down to a science with my cooking on Thursday after rehearsal and the big party at the theater for seventy or eighty people on Friday night after the taping. I'll never forget how wonderful the whole thing made me feel. Doing that cooking was a small way of showing the gratitude I felt for all of the talented and dedicated people who worked so hard to make my show successful.

PEARL'S RICE PUDDING

You will figure out how you like it best—how sweet and how thick. Here are the things that go in there: 3 or 4 cups cooked rice; milk (use quite a bit the first time, then work back down if necessary);

1 large box raisins; vanilla (use a lot, because it's weaker than it used to be); 4 to 6 eggs; ¼ pound butter; sugar, as much as you like. I use *plenty.*

After precooking the rice, put it into a roast pan or large casserole. Mix in all other ingredients—just put them all in there at once, Honey. Stir well and put into a 350° oven for about 40 minutes. Remember, the more milk you use, the better the pudding will hold its moisture until the next day.

Keeping up with the rehearsals and taping a weekly TV variety hour is a pretty strenuous exercise for everybody concerned. Often people will start to get tired and irritable in a situation like that. I think part of the problem comes from the fact that they are not *eating* properly or regularly. Louis passed along a little trick to all. Mix about equal parts of peanuts, mints, and raisins. I used to keep little containers of the mixture around the theater and in the offices so that people could just grab a handful and munch. I think it did a lot for everybody concerned. I think some were even putting on weight, despite the schedule we were keeping.

Bob Finkel was my producer. When his birthday rolled around I dreamed up a special treat for him. I had some of the office people empty out a waste basket and wash it with ammonia. Then I lined it with beautiful paper and filled that whole thing up with the special mixture. It took a couple of guys to get that thing in Bob's office. We had a real good laugh, and he started nibbling right away.

Almost a year after Bing was a guest on my show I taped a special with him. Again, we were rehearsing during the week for a Friday night taping. I kidded Bing, telling him that he shouldn't plan on dinner Friday night because I was bringing that wonderful meal again. We laughed and I don't think he took me seriously.

Well, Thursday night as I started home from the studio in the car I was thinking about what I could cook for Bing, because I really meant to go through with it. I knew that I would not be cooking just for him, because for sure there would be a few others around. Just before I stopped at the market I opened my purse and counted out exactly thirteen dollars. That was it. I had wanted to cook for six or eight people because I knew good and well that the director and maybe some of the writers would smell that food and want to try a little bit.

I went into the market with my thirteen dollars and decided to see how I could make that work. I picked up six sweet potatoes, but they weighed too much. I put them down and picked up four. I figured I could cut them in half if I had to after Bing had a whole one. Then I thought, "Gee, I'll pass by the meat counter now so I can lay a couple of ham hocks on Bing." I asked for four, but when we got them on the scale it turned out that I was only going to buy two. Don't forget, I had my thirteen dollars measured out pretty well. I picked up some string beans and then I was still trying to figure out what to do about meat. I figured chicken was about the cheapest thing I could buy, and I did want to have plenty. I picked up three cut-up chickens. When I got to the cash register, I was holding my breath. It came out to $12.83 with tax.

Friday night after the show, I made a grand ceremony out of opening up that meal for Bing. He just expressed his approval, put his pipe down, and wiped out everything.

SMOKED TROUT
(Bing Crosby)

I've already told you that he loves to fish. You may be interested then to know what he does with trout. I will give it to you just as he gave it to me:

"More delicate flavor than lox and great for snacks. For this you need a piscatorial enthusiast and a hobby carpenter to make you a smoke box. This is a tight wooden box about 2' x 2' x 4' tall, with a front open flap to fit over your outdoor cooker.

"Clean the fish without cutting the throats, so they

can hang on a crossbar several inches from the box top. Soak them overnight in a brine heavy enough to float an egg. The next morning, with the box open, cook the fish over a wood fire 1½ to 2 hours, or until the skin hardens. Then, using green willows over the fire, close the box and cover with a tarpaulin to retain the smoke. Depending on the cure you like, 2 or 3 hours of slow smoking should suffice."

COMPOTE OF GAME BIRDS
(*Bing Crosby*)

In the same letter, Bing gave me another recipe that sounds just wonderful:

"First capture yourself a Nimrod! You need pheasant, duck, and quail in stew proportions, with ham and sweetbread if you like.

"Start by boiling the bones with celery, carrots, onions, etc. Strain and add the meat. Cook slowly in Madeira sauce. Add sweetbreads during the last 15 minutes of cooking.

"The sauce is ½ *Español*, ½ tomato sauce and Madeira wine. Fear not the alcohol, which boils out, leaving only flavor. If you decide to make your own *Español* sauce, it takes 2 days. So get it in a can at the gourmet store. Serve this dish with ½ wild rice and ½ brown rice, or all wild rice if you prefer. I find that the brown rice adds body.

"Meringue Glacé makes a fine dessert. But careful, Pearlie, it's fattening!"

Actually, making my money stretch was just like the old days when all the performers on a job might toss in a dime or fifteen cents each in order to get up a pot of something to eat. I think really if you have ever had to develop an eye for economy you never lose it, no matter how your circumstances may change. I don't have to play it too close these days, of course, because things have worked out pretty well for us.

I do think that some people believe that people like us have more money than we really have. When prices go up it seems to me that they hit us the hardest. I have stage dresses that cost twenty dollars to have cleaned. Then there's travel expense and all the rest. There is a staff to think about. Anyhow, I'm not complaining, I'm just trying to point out that I still look at the prices when I go to the supermarket. If you find things out of place in the store, dear friend, it just may be because Pearlie, or somebody like her, has been in there before you. Sometimes I'll pick up something without looking at the price. Then when I find out how much it costs, I put it right out of my basket wherever I happen to be. There is a kind of principle involved, and a reflex from the past.

ARROZ CON POLLO
(Rose Tizol)

Speaking of the past brings another wonderful cook to mind.

Rose and Juan Tizol had a room for rent in their home in California. Before we met, Louis and I each rented that room for a time. The Tizols liked and remembered us both, and actually helped to bring us together. I still consider Rose to be a very dear friend.

Here is Rose's magical way with a chicken. Start with these ingredients: 1 3½-pound fryer, 1 tablespoon oil, 2 small onions, 1 green pepper, about 1 dozen capers (no more), 6 green olives, 1 small can pimentos, sliced, 2 stalks of celery, ½ small can tomato sauce, ½ cup water, 1½ cups rice.

Brown the chicken slightly in oil. Slice the onions, celery, and green peppers into small pieces. Lay them on top of the chicken. Turn off the gas for about ½ hour and let it sit.

Slice the olives and pimentos and lay them on top of the onions and green peppers, along with capers, tomato sauce, and water. Let it cook for

½ hour. Wash the rice very well. Then stir it into this mixture and continue to cook until the rice is done.

SOUR CREAM POUND CAKE
(Rose Tizol)

The ingredients are: ½ cup butter, 3 cups cake flour, 1 cup sour cream, 3 teaspoons vanilla, 5 eggs, 3 teaspoons baking powder.

Cream the butter and sugar. Beat in 1 egg at a time. Then add the sour cream. Finally, mix baking powder with the flour and add small portions of flour at a time as you stir. Oil and flour a cake pan with a hole in the middle. Cook about 50 minutes in a 325° oven.

BLACK BEANS
(Rose Tizol)

The ingredients are: 2 ham hocks, 1 pound black beans, 1 large onion, 1 large green pepper, 1 clove of garlic (mashed), and salt.

Cook ham hocks, *not until done,* but for only 1 hour. Wash the beans in cold water. Put enough cold water in the pan to just cover the beans. Bring to a slow boil. Then pour beans and water into the pot with the ham hocks. Cook slowly until soft.

These beans may be served with rice and a tossed salad. By the way, black beans can be purchased at any Latin-American grocery.

During the hardest times, as I look back on it, the key to everything was maintaining a certain *dignity.* I've worked in vaudeville, legitimate theater, movies, and cabarets. I suppose that there are possibilities for indignity in any of that, no matter how much *money* you are making. I suppose that legitimate stage is the most dignified and demanding. Unlike vaudeville, there are other performers out there, and you have to interact with them quite a lot. You form a kind of group and you have to match your parts in the play as well as your personalities backstage. In vaudeville, by contrast, you're usually out there alone. And when you go backstage you don't much care whether you get along with all the other performers or not. The thing that matters is how you affect the audience when you are on. Now I'm going to give you recipes from a couple of fellows who know that tradition, and who have no trouble at all in relating to an audience.

ROCK CORNISH HENS
(Victor Borge)

Once upon a time, Denmark was very kind to America. It sent us a warm, extremely talented man. We fell in love with him over here, and the love affair has continued through the years. He is Victor Borge.

He can be a very funny man for sure, but one thing definitely is not a joke with him. He goes crazy for Rock Cornish hens, properly prepared. I'm proud to get his favorite recipe here. Note, please, that these hens are treated to musical entertainment while they're in the oven!

"Rub the insides of 6 Rock Cornish pullets with salt and pepper. Sear in ¼ pound butter in Dutch oven until golden brown—10 to 12 minutes. (If a clock is not available, all you've got to do is play the 'Minute Waltz' 10 to 12 times.) Add 1¼ cups of water and let simmer, covered, until tender—approximately 35 minutes. (Here, the 'Dance of the Hours' played ½ through will come in handy, if dragged slightly.) Remove birds. Stir like crazy into drippings a paste of cold water and 3 teaspoons of flour. Add ½ cup light cream, salt, tasteless sauce coloring, and ½ teaspoon sugar. Serves 6."

For years, people have asked Victor why he doesn't finish some of the piano pieces he starts. As for me, I love his artistry. So it always gives me, personally, a glow to know a talent who can, but does not *have* to finish a song. He fills us so that we are not cheated. I get the feeling that he is a performer who lets himself go and tosses in an extra dash of this and that just for the special amusement of himself and his audience. I wouldn't be surprised to find that he takes the same approach to cooking. An extra dash of spice once in a while can't really destroy the goodness of a basic dish. The main thing is that Victor Borge is always *giving,* and that's *living,* and that's *loving.*

LASAGNA
(Tony Bennett)

Tony Bennett's *heart* may be in San Francisco, but his *appetite* is still at its best at his own Mama's table. I knew Tony when he really was still Mrs. Benedetto's little boy. Ever since that time, we have had the closest personal and professional respect for one another. Mrs. Benedetto has generously given me her recipe for Tony's favorite lasagna. I think you'll like it.

The recipe is for 2 trays of lasagna, serving about 10 people. You begin by making that wonderful sauce. Get some Italian sausage and loosen the meat inside. Strain 1 large and 1 small can of tomatoes. Put all of this into a pot on the stove and add 1 large can of tomato *purée,* plus one large can of tomato *paste.* Season with garlic powder, basil leaves, and a little cinnamon. Now add 1 to 1½ pounds ground meat fried with chopped onions.

Boil 2 boxes of lasagna, adding a little oil to the water when you boil it to prevent lasagna from sticking. When lasagna is done, drain it.

Mix together ricotta cheese and 5 eggs.

Build the lasagna as follows. Put sauce on the bottom of the tray, then a layer of lasagna, then a layer of ricotta and eggs, then a layer of grated cheese and another layer of sauce and so forth. Bake

in 350° oven for ¾ of an hour. Then remove and
let it stand for a few minutes before serving.

I think that a lot of the forms of entertainment
that have come along since the legitimate theater
passed through its heyday have cheapened the performing art a bit.
Television, for example, really is, at its worst, a
boob tube. It too seldom offers any real intelligence
or wit to the people who watch it. In my case, I
asked the industry why in the hell we couldn't go
back to *entertaining* people with a little black
box instead of worrying so much about the *ratings.*
Programing people in television are so careful and
calculating.
I wonder if pay TV wouldn't be better, so that
people could actually pick up the tab for the things
that they need and want. I don't say that we should
do away with free TV, but I think that pay TV
might be a welcome addition to the scene. We need
good musical plays, dramas, and variety shows without the intervention of ratings (which may or may
not be correct in the first place). Without any question, I think that the rating system is full of—well,
I guess I won't say the word in a cookbook. My
favorite TV people are those who are so solid as
professionals that they transcend the mediocre
tendencies of the business—people who can make it
with or without TV.

MEAT LOAF
(Carol Burnett)

This lady is one of my real favorites. Like all good
comediennes or comedians, she has a touch of
seriousness about her. She is one of those performers
who has managed to remain herself even as she has
become a very big star. That, I think, is always the
mark of a true professional and a solid person.
I asked Carol if she had a favorite recipe she
might submit for the book. At first she said no, she

really didn't do any cooking to speak of. But she says that she does make a pretty good meat loaf. Here's how it goes.

Ingredients: 2 pounds ground round, 2 eggs, 2 cans tomato sauce (8 oz. cans), milk, chopped onion, chopped pepper (green), bread crumbs, salt, pepper, onion salt, garlic salt.

"Beat eggs with a little bit of milk in a bowl. Add 1 can tomato sauce and beat. Add onion and peppers, and squish the meat with hands through all this mess (wash hands first). Add salt, pepper, etc., to taste. Add a few bread crumbs to hold it all together and pat into loaf. Place loaf in electric frying pan with a little oil. Pour over remaining tomato sauce. Cook about 1½ hours at 325°."

See, *all* great cooks make up words. Carol "squishes the meat with hands." Sounds just like her!

BURT'S BEEF STEW
(Burt Reynolds)

Well, would you believe that with a physique like that he can also cook? This is a talented guy. He has made some beautiful movies. He has been a weekly host for the Tonight Show, and when you see him on a dinner dais, he is always in fantastic form with that sense of humor. Here's what you will need for Burt's Beef Stew: 3 slices of bacon cut into small pieces, 2 pounds lean beef (chuck is juicy) cut into 1" cubes, flour (enough to cover meat), salt and pepper to taste, 1 tablespoon sugar, a few dashes monosodium glutamate, 1 onion, 1 clove garlic, 6 ounces tomato sauce, 1 cup dry Burgundy wine, 2 carrots cut up coarsely, 2 stalks celery cut up coarsely, 2 large potatoes cut into quarters, ½ cup fresh mushrooms, 1 bay leaf (if you like it), pinch of thyme, ½ can beef broth, or water.

Cook the bacon in a large heavy pot. Salt and pepper the beef and dip it in flour. Brown it in bacon fat, turning often. Add a little oil if needed. Sprinkle with sugar. Add onion, garlic, and brown a little. Add tomato sauce, water or broth, wine, bay leaf, and thyme. Cover and cook slowly for about 1½ hours. Add carrots, celery, then potatoes and mushrooms. Uncover and cook until meat and vegetables are tender.

CHILI
(Foster Brooks)

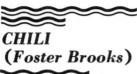

Foster and I became good friends through Bill Cosby. He has worked with Cosby on a number of dates, and recently both Foster and I appeared on a Bill Cosby show. Foster's special trademark is his impression of a drunk. He must be the best in the whole business.

Naturally, when we were rehearsing and taping the show, Foster and I would take odd moments to talk, and naturally the subject eventually turned to cooking. I'm glad it did too, because it turns out that Foster has a superb recipe for chili. You know, chili can be very, very good or very, very bad. Once and for all, let Foster tell you how to do it the right way.

"I start out by putting about 4 pounds of lean ground beef in a big pot. I break it up as it cooks, and when all the red has gone out of it I drain off any grease that has formed in the pan.

"Then I open 1 can of tomatoes, cut the hard core out of each piece, and pour the tomatoes into a bowl and crush them into little bitty pieces. I add the tomatoes, along with 1 large diced onion, to the meat. Right at this point, I also salt the meat a bit.

"Next, I add 2 4-ounce cans of good diced chilies. Mix everything real good and add a little water. Simmer this mixture for a while, so that the onions and tomatoes can cook a bit with the meat and the chilies. Keep the lid on while you do this.

"Now open 2 small cans of tomato *paste,* 1 large can of tomato *purée,* and 1, 2, 3, 4 or more medium cans of Hunt's small red beans. You will have to be the judge of how many beans you like in your chili. You may also choose to use a different *kind* of bean. Some folks prefer kidney beans, some pinto. Use whatever you want, and as much as you want.

"Add the tomato paste first to the meat and mix well. Rinse the cans with a little water and pour that in too. Next, add at least 3 heaping tablespoons of chili powder. (I prefer Spice Island brand.) And if you can get it, 2 tablespoons of chili con carne powder. Then, 2 tablespoons of ground cumin and 1 heaping tablespoon of sugar. Mix this all up very well.

"Then add the tomato purée and beans. Again, rinse the purée can with water and pour that in. Mix thoroughly. Allow to simmer until the chili reaches the desired thickness. You may have to add a bit of salt to taste. Sometimes, I add chili pequins, which are tiny dried peppers. If you can get them, just crush 5 or 6 in your hand and stir into the chili as it cooks. They add a delicious flavor and a pleasant 'hot' to the chili.

"You do all this, and I am sure you will receive raves about your delicious chili, as I have many times. And when someone asks how you make it, just tell them it's an old family recipe and that it was handed down to you from a high shelf in your kitchen by a friend of yours who could reach it better than you could. I hope you like it."

Like most performers, and more so than some, I kind of resent the person who criticizes for the sake of criticizing. In any field of human activity a specialist should be left to his job the best he can. You have to have a certain trust in a person who has chosen a particular field for his activity. The layman does not instruct the surgeon in the use of knives. The man off the street who needs heels on his shoes does not tell the cobbler how to put them on. If the cobbler stands there tapping away with his little hammer and you continue to tell him how you want your heels put on, he might be justified in handing the shoes right back to you without do-ing a thing. It's not that he's so busy, it's just that *you* do not really have a right to tell him how to practice his profession. Your place is to tell him what you want done and then accept the products of his labors.

You know that I have to mention critics here. Critics can *season* a show, and they *burn* quite a few too.

I guess it sounds as if I hate all journalists who write about our business, but that's far from the truth. I have a number of really good friends among the folks who report on our business. There were a couple of them whose recipes just had to be in here.

PANNED STUFFING
A LA ROSEMARY
(*Rosemary Wilson*)

Rosemary is a fine cook, and her husband, Earl (the columnist), is very appreciative of that fact. I asked Rosemary for a recipe, hoping to get something that would be a favorite of Earl's. She replied in a note, "Here is the recipe for Earl's favorite stuffing. I hope it's something you can use in your book. I'm pleased and flattered that you asked me.

"The recipe is a stuffing for turkey, chicken, or pork. Start with 1 loaf of stale bread, 2 medium green peppers diced, ½ cup celery diced, 1 large onion diced, 2 or 3 tablespoons of butter, a generous pinch of sage (or more, according to your own taste), salt and pepper.

"Tear the bread apart and put it in a colander. Run cold water over it (not too much) to soften the bread. Let it drip while you cook vegetables in a large frying pan in butter until they are soft but not brown. Stir often.

"Now press the water out of the bread and mix with vegetables in the frying pan. You may add more butter if needed to make the mixing easier. Add sage, salt, and pepper. Spoon off just enough juices from the roasting pan (in which you are baking your turkey or chicken) to make gravy later.

Put stuffing into the remaining juices in the roasting pan and mix them into the stuffing as you would mix a salad.

"Bake 20 minutes to ½ hour, either with the turkey or by itself. It should be slightly brown on top and not soggy.

"When I do this with chicken or turkey, I usually boil the neck, liver, gizzard, etc., to get a good flavored broth for the gravy. I take a small amount of the broth, about ½ cup, and mix it into the stuffing when I'm mixing the bread and vegetables. It adds extra flavor, but it isn't absolutely necessary."

MEXICAN CHOCOLATE CAKE
(Maxine Mesinger)

Maxine writes for the Houston *Chronicle,* and she is one of those people I love so much that I think of them as family. Maxine, to me, seems like a sister. She is one heck of a cook too, and I am going to pass along 3 of her favorites.

For the Mexican Chocolate Cake, melt together in a saucepan: 1 stick margarine, ½ cup vegetable or corn oil, 2 squares unsweetened chocolate (or 4 tablespoons cocoa), and 1 cup water.

Now mix together the following in a large bowl: 2 cups flour, 2 cups sugar, ½ cup sour milk, 2 beaten eggs, 1 teaspoon vanilla, 1 teaspoon soda. Optional—1 teaspoon cinnamon. This is what gives it the Mexican chocolate flavor. Then add the first mixture and beat until well mixed.

Pour the batter into a greased sheath pan 12" x 18". Bake 20 to 25 minutes at 350°.

Five minutes before the cake is done, start making icing. Heat together until it bubbles around the edge: 1 stick margarine, 2 squares chocolate (or 4 tablespoons cocoa), 6 tablespoons milk. Remove from heat and add: 1 box confectioners sugar, 1 teaspoon vanilla, 1½ cups chopped pecans (or decorate the top with pecan halves). Beat until creamy, and ice the cake when it comes out of the oven, still hot.

BAKED STEAK
(Maxine Mesinger)

Mix together in a saucepan: ¾ cup tomato ketchup, 3 tablespoons Worcestershire sauce, ½ cup margarine, 1 tablespoon lemon juice.

Slice 1 or 2 onions about ¼" thick so that you have enough slices to cover the top of the steak. You will also need 5 cloves of garlic, or as many as it takes to cover one side of the steak. Finally, you will need enough fresh mushrooms to cover the steak.

Season 1 side of the steak with salt and pepper. Put it under a broiler until it's good and brown on that side. Remove the steak from the broiler. Turn the uncooked side up. Salt and pepper to taste. Put garlic through a garlic press and rub the uncooked side of the steak. Put onion slices on top of the steak, then pour mixture from the sauce pan over it. Add fresh mushrooms. Bake at 350°: very rare—1 hour; medium rare—1¼ hours; well done—1½ hours.

SQUASH AND CHEESE CASSEROLE
(Maxine Mesinger)

To serve 10 people, use the following ingredients: 3 pounds yellow squash, 8 egg yolks, 1½ cups grated American cheese, 2 cups cottage cheese, 1½ cups white bread crumbs, 1 heaping tablespoon of butter or margarine, ½ cup grated onion, salt, white pepper, nutmeg, and sugar to taste.

Sauté onions in butter until lightly cooked. Slice squash and add to onion. Cover pan and steam until squash is done. Add bread crumbs, American and cottage cheese. Mix well over low fire. When cheeses are totally melted, add salt, pepper, nutmeg, and sugar to taste. Add beaten egg yolks to mixture and mix well. Transfer to greased casserole (8½" x 12½") and bake for 30 minutes at 350°.

POTATO SPICE CAKE
(Mrs. G. W. Holt)

Mrs. Holt is one of the most devoted of my fans. Audiences, after all, may be the most important of *all* critics. She lives in Ventura, California, with her husband and two of her sons. The other two sons are married. Not too long ago Mrs. Holt and her husband, celebrating their thirtieth anniversary, went to a performance of *Hello, Dolly!* Then, more recently, Mrs. Holt heard me mention on television (or somewhere) that I was working on a third book, a cookbook. I received a long and thoughtful letter full of love. At the end was included a recipe for a delicious potato cake. I want to include it because I know this lady is an excellent wife, mother, and cook.

Ingredients: 2 cups flour, 2 cups sugar, ¾ cup shortening, 4 eggs, separated, ¼ cup cocoa, ½ teaspoon cloves, 1 teaspoon cinnamon, 1 teaspoon nutmeg, 2 teaspoons soda, 2 cups mashed potatoes, 1 cup sour milk, 2 cups raisins, 2 cups nuts, if desired, 1 teaspoon of vanilla.

Cream the sugar, shortening, and egg yolks. Add mashed potatoes and beat well. Add flour, spices, soda, and cocoa alternately with sour milk. Add vanilla, nuts, and raisins. Finally, fold in the stiffly beaten egg whites and bake in a greased oblong pan at 350° for 45 minutes.

CRAB-APPLE JELLY
CRAB-APPLE BUTTER
(Grace Gilbert)

This lady is another of the most ardent fans I have ever had. In her kitchen, in Toledo, she cooks the old-fashioned way. In the letter that accompanied these recipes she said, "Except for the sugar, I don't measure. Even the amount of cider used depends on the juiciness of the pulp and how long it is refrigerated before I 'put it up.' "

Canning and preserving are great arts. It seems to me that those arts have pretty much passed out of existence in the average American kitchen. Still, I remember from my Mama's kitchen that it's a beautiful thing to be able to reach up on a shelf and pull down home-canned peaches or preserves, pickled corn or watermelon rind. I never mastered that art, but Mama was very good at it. I'm glad to have Miss Gilbert's recipes in this book.

As you will see, Miss Gilbert gets crab-apple butter and crab-apple jelly out of the same crab apples. Her recipe gives the basic facts, but leaves out the quantities. That means that you are going to have to do a little experimenting and practicing along the way. Here is how she tells it:

"Wash, cut up, and core crab apples, being sure all blemishes on skins are removed. Put in large pan, cover with water, and bring to boil. Boil lightly until apples begin to soften. Pour in cheesecloth laid over a large bowl. Tie up firmly. Let drip until most of the juice is in the bowl. Bottle the juice. Refrigerate if not to be cooked immediately. Put apples through colander. Refrigerate pulp if necessary. (Apple skins can be composted.)

"Apple Jelly: Put juice in large, deep pan. Add ⅔ cup of sugar for each cup of juice. Use moderate heat. Stir in sugar. Stir continually to keep from sticking. Skim constantly until clear. Lemon juice may be added toward the end if desired. Test steadily as jelly thickens. When 2 drops form and hold on spoon, pour into glasses. Mint leaf may be placed on top if desired. Loosen *slightly* around edge of glass when hot, and cover with paraffin wax.

"Apple Butter: Use ½ cup brown sugar, the darker the better, to 1 cup of pulp. Use a *deep* pan, as butter plops upward while cooking. A wooden spoon with a long handle is best for stirring. Add about 1 cup of fresh cider for 1 quart of pulp.

More may be needed later if butter becomes too thick before being done. Use moderate heat, cook slowly, and stir constantly. When about done add spices, usually ginger, cinnamon, nutmeg, and all-spice, and nuts as desired. The butter is done when it is rather smooth on top, and tastes right. Fill jars to the top. Put caps on rather loosely at first, and tighten firmly when jars are cool.

"A jelly bag for dripping can be made by laying cheesecloth over a large bowl or container, looping a stout cord with a slipknot around the bowl, and drawing it up over the cheesecloth after the apple contents have been poured in, being sure that all edges of the cheesecloth are held firmly in the tightened knot. The handle of a cupboard door, if at the right height, may be used to tie the bag if the cord is looped twice over the handle, and the end of the cord tied around both loops and around the ends of the tied cheesecloth. This will hold about 3 quarts of cooked apples and juice."

STREUSEL SPICE CAKE
(Rose DeDominicis)

Now I have a surprise for you. Mrs. Carl DeDo-minicis, "Rose" to me now, has kindly agreed to let me include her recipe for her prize-winning cake. This particular recipe, from a terrific cook, won the $25,000 grand prize in Pillsbury Company's Bake-Off Number 23. According to Rose, she has been a fan of mine for quite some time. Now that I have this recipe, I am definitely a fan of hers.

"Ingredients: 1 package Pillsbury Yellow Cre-ate-A-Cake Mix, ¾ cup milk or water (I use milk), ½ cup butter or margarine melted (prefer butter), 4 eggs, ½ cup flaked coconut, ½ cup chopped nuts, 1 envelope premelted chocolate, or 1-ounce square unsweetened chocolate, melted.

"Filling: ½ cup flaked coconut, ½ cup chopped nuts, ½ cup firmly packed brown sugar, 2 table-spoons flour, 2 tablespoons cinnamon.

"Glaze: 1 cup powdered sugar, 1 tablespoon butter or margarine, softened, 2 to 3 tablespoons milk.

"Preheat oven to 350° (325° for pan with colored outer surface). Grease and flour 10" tube or Bundt pan. Blend first 4 ingredients in large bowl until moistened; beat as directed on package. Stir in coconut and nuts. Marble chocolate throughout batter. Pour ½ batter (about 2 cups) into pan. Combine in small bowl all filling ingredients. Sprinkle ¾ over batter in pan. Cover with remaining batter; sprinkle with remaining filling. Bake at 350° for 45 to 55 minutes, until top springs back when touched lightly in center. Cool upright in pan 30 minutes; remove from pan. Cool. Blend in small bowl. Glaze ingredients until smooth. Glaze cake."

When you find a performer who has made a name for himself in our business while maintaining his integrity and his evenness of mind, you have found a real solid person. These are the people I respect in show business and the people I love as dear friends. Some of their recipes had to be in this book.

One of those people is Tony Pastor, the great saxophonist and band leader. I've known Tony for many years. He and I once made a record together called "Put the Blame on Mame." That one must go back twenty years. I didn't see Tony for a while, and then one day a very nice man from legitimate theater, Jack Schlissel, asked me to see three young boys sing. They turned out to be Tony's sons. What a beautiful sound they made. It sounded like some of the groups that were on the way up when I was young. The special flavor and the true harmony were there. The boys worked with me on quite a few jobs.

In addition to being a fine performer, Tony, Jr., turned out to be an active writer and quite a gourmet. I'm going to pass along some of Tony's best concoctions, but I have to warn you first that they're going to be fairly expensive to prepare. Not heavily expensive, but moderately so. Tony lives as a bachelor, so I guess he can afford to spend a little more money at the store. Then too, maybe it helps to attract the females. Cooking is one of the things that he cares about, and he simply doesn't go halfway with it. Look at the recipes and you can be the judge about whether you can afford the time and money to prepare these wonderful dishes.

SCALLOPINI DI NINO
(Tony Pastor)

You start with 6 very thin veal cutlets and pound them in order to make them as thin as possible. Season them with salt and pepper, and brown them in 3 tablespoons of butter on both sides. Add 1½ cups of cooked peas, 1 cup of sliced mushrooms, and 6 slices of very lean ham. Finally, pour in 1 cup of dry white wine, and 2 or 3 more tablespoons of butter. Simmer for 10 minutes. That one doesn't really sound too complicated after all.

POLO À LA PASTOR
(Tony Pastor)

Have 2 good frying chickens cut into pieces. Salt and pepper them, and assemble the additional ingredients: ¼ cup of oil, 1 small finely chopped onion, 1 cup of dry white wine, 1 pound of fresh peeled tomato, 4 green peppers cut in slices, and 1 crushed garlic clove. Now, when you have rubbed the chicken with salt and pepper, heat the oil in a skillet. Sauté the chicken until it is golden brown on all sides and add the onion and white wine. Cook this mixture until the wine has been reduced by ½, then add tomatoes and continue the cooking. Meanwhile, in another skillet, sauté green peppers with the fresh garlic and oil. Add this to the chicken and cook until the chicken is done. Now that one starts to get a little more challenging.

ANTIPASTO À LA PASTOR
(Tony Pastor)

This one is out of this world! Get some shrimp, clams, and mussels, about 15 of each. Then get 4 very tender baby squid. Substitute scallops for the squid if you prefer. If the shrimp is unshelled, boil it, cool it, and remove the shells. Steam the clams and mussels and remove from the shells. Clean and cut the squid into little pieces. Cook the pieces in seasoned water till tender. If scallops are used, steam them for about 5 minutes in salted water with lemon peel and chopped onion. Then cut in slices. Cool the fish in the refrigerator, then marinate the fish in oil, lemon juice, crushed garlic, and salt and pepper for about an hour before serving. Then grunt, and groan, and suffer, and taste, and enjoy!

PEPPERONI DE JUNIOR
(Tony Pastor)

It seems as though Tony named this one after himself. I think he figures this one is the masterpiece.

You will need 2 slices of white bread (without crust) soaking in milk or water, 6 green peppers, salt and pepper, 1½ cups of tuna fish, 12 black pitted olives cut into pieces, and oil. You cut off the tops of the peppers and scoop out the seeds. Make a mixture of the bread, salt, pepper, tuna fish, and olives and stuff the peppers with that. Top each pepper with oil and place them in a well-oiled casserole, covered tightly. Bake in a moderate oven for about 45 minutes to an hour. If you wish, you may top the peppers with grated cheese during the last 15 minutes of cooking time.

A recipe like that ought to get Tony thousands of proposals of marriage. All I can say is that I hope he marries a girl who is either as good a cook as he is or else is no cook at all. Anything in-between could produce arguments in that household.

In *Hello, Dolly!* there's a scene where Dolly Levi, the lady whose part I played, has to do a pretty convincing job of eating a chicken dinner on the stage. That means that when I was in *Dolly!* I had to eat that chicken *eight times a week*—six nights and twice on Sunday. Along the way, I had some pretty good baked chicken and some pretty bad baked chicken. As a matter of fact, up on that stage, although I had to eat as though I loved every morsel, I have had some of the *worst* baked chicken the world has ever seen!

One night, I remember biting into a breast of chicken and finding it almost completely raw down near the bone. Now don't forget, I already had a mouthful of this, because the scene called for me to eat fast, and with questionable table manners. Well, I had to continue the scene, although nothing destroys me more than raw chicken. After this scene was over, there was hell to pay.

People usually think of me as a fairly decent person to work with. Mostly gentle and nice. Well, here came some evidence that there was the other side in me, too. When I stepped out into the wings after working on that chicken in front of all those people, I must have been burning at white heat. They could have heard me anywhere within six blocks of the St. James Theater. After that, when we took the show on the road, I had lots of different cooks in lots of different towns preparing baked chicken for me. In a new location I never knew exactly what to expect, but I was a little more cautious with those first couple of bites in a new town.

The same plate in the same scene also had to have some big dumplings on it. According to our script, I was supposed to be eating chicken and dumplings. I played the dumpling bit with cotton

candy. I was supposed to reach down and get myself
a dumpling and start sopping up gravy. That was
a funny bit because I was sitting in an elegant
restaurant at the time. That is what Dolly would
do under the circumstances. I remember one night
after the show I was having what I called my "Act
Three," where I talked and kidded around with the
audience after the last curtain. I revealed to a little
child the secret of my dumpling. I looked down at
him and said, "I can just look at you and tell that
you liked the dumpling part, didn't you?" The
child was drizzling at the mouth. He said, "Oh,
Miss Bailey, I wish I could have had some of those
dumplings." I said, "Well, sweetheart, they weren't
really dumplings, they were cotton candy." And
with that his little face lighted up and his mouth
started drizzling even more. I said, "I suppose you
think *you* would like to have cotton candy dumplings." And he said yes, yes he would. I said, "But
how about trying that eight times a week?" He
said, "That would be wonderful." I figured, okay,
great, because a little child never seems to get tired
of sweet stuff. I said to him "That's great for you
because when all your little baby teeth fall out
from eating sweets, you'll get new ones to replace
them. But if Miss Bailey has her teeth fall out, she
has to go buy them back."

By the way, did you catch that word *sopping?*
How many of you know that word? How many of
you knew it before you read this book? Okay, hands
down. I was surprised during the run of *Dolly!* to
find that a lot of people were not familiar with
that word. They thought it meant something like
the same think as *dunking,* which, of course, it does
not. A lady came to me after the show one night
and said, "I thought that was so cute the way you
dunked your dumpling." I said, "Dear heart, thank
you, but I was sopping my plate."

I have to laugh when I think back on it now.
Many, many years ago when I was just a kid,
everybody in my neighborhood knew what sopping
meant. Adults would take some syrup or molasses,

thin it a little bit with bacon grease, and warm it. Then the little kids would get half a biscuit and sop that mixture up. It may sound horrible to you now, but it was a very delicious taste. Have a charity dinner on that one today, and bring limousines in from all over. Next thing you know the price of molasses will go sky high!

ZUCCHINI BLOSSOMS
(*Arlene Liff*)

Samuel "Biff" Liff was Production Manager of *Hello, Dolly!* when I was with the show. Then, when I had to go into the hospital with heart trouble, I received a shoe box. I remember thinking that it seemed an unusual gift for someone in the hospital. Inside, I found beautiful tomatoes, parsnips, and flowers from the Liffs' garden out in Yonkers. What a beautiful surprise that was! Arlene knows what to *do* with good food, too, once she has grown it. I guess she has it easy getting her hands on zucchini blossoms. The rest of you are on your own.

I'm going to give you several of Arlene's recipes just as she gave them to me. Something of her delightful personality comes through in the way she writes her recipes. First the blossoms:

"This is a smashing tidbit for the cocktail hour, or served as a vegetable. The blossom is like the concentrated essence of zucchini.

"*Now*—find a big zucchini patch and pick 6 full blossoms per serving. This is the hardest part!

"Dunk each blossom in batter: ½ cup milk and 1 egg blended with 2 tablespoons of flour, or use pancake mix, thinned.

"Now think of them as French fries as you toss blossoms into a pot of very hot cooking oil. Turn them gently as they brown very slightly.

"Lift out of oil with slotted spoon. Drain briefly on paper towels. Let each guest salt his own serving."

CHOCOLATE MOUSSE
(Arlene Liff)

You need: 1 package chocolate bits (6 to 8 oz.), melted over hot water. Separate 2 eggs, and beat the yolks as though for scrambled eggs with 1 *whole* egg. Stir into chocolate. Beat the 2 remaining egg whites very stiff, and fold into chocolate mix. Beat ½ pint heavy cream and fold into chocolate mix. Pour into 8" spring-form lined with 24 lady fingers, split. (First, line bottom of form. Then line wall of form with fingers standing on end. Snip off rounded ends to steady them.)

Refrigerate for 4 hours. Can be held overnight.

Serve with thin topping of whipped cream and chocolate curls shaved from Dutch bittersweet bar. Preparation time 45 minutes. Serves 8 to 10 people.

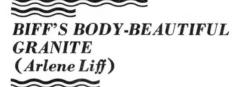

BIFF'S BODY-BEAUTIFUL GRANITE
(Arlene Liff)

"This dessert is the dieter's delight. Biff has added the booze flavors . . . and as usual, he's right!

"Put into your blender and whiz: 2 to 3 cups of fruit with its juice (diet canned or fresh). Juice added to equal 1 quart. Liquid Sucaryl: double the amount you think is enough, because the sweet taste weakens in the freezing tray. (And oversweet is what our little fat hearts crave!) Pour into ice-cube trays. Stir in 2 jiggers of booze or liquor-flavored extract. Freeze approximately 1 hour. Create your own combinations or try ours:

Fruit	Juice	Booze
Peaches	Papaya or orange	Brandy
Cherries	Cranberry	Rum
Apricots	Orange	Brandy
Strawberries	Apple	Kirsch

After *Dolly!* I swore that I never wanted to look at another bird in my whole life, least of all a *chicken.* Lately, though, after a little respite, I have gone back to chicken. I just love chicken and fish. The wonderful thing is that I do not put on weight when I eat them. The reason is that they have practically no fat in them at all. I even take the skin off chicken, and never miss it. Veal is good for dieting too. The doctor who wants me to keep my weight down is well pleased. And frankly, I never go hungry.

My co-star in *Dolly!,* the man who played Horace Vandergelder, was the great Cab Calloway. He and his beautiful wife, Nuffy, make a regular ritual out of the Sunday-afternoon barbecue up in White Plains. After Cab works all week, and he works as hard as anybody, he loves to have that large family of children and grandchildren come around him for a barbecue dinner. He sits over that congregation like a mother hen.

I went up there one Sunday afternoon. There must have been twenty or thirty people there when I got there. I remember the beautiful Roy Campanella, one of Cab's neighbors, was on hand for the barbecue. And there, amid family, friends, show-business associates, and neighbors was Cab dishing out the food.

I have a quick and simple recipe for cooking spareribs. It doesn't involve a barbecue, but it's certainly delicious just the same.

SPARERIBS SIMPLE
(*My Recipe*)

I start with either the country spareribs or the regular long ones. If I decide to use a pot on top of the stove, I put the spareribs in about ½ pot of water, or I at least make sure they are completely covered. It's important to use a kind of large pot. I boil that until I see the water starting to boil down, then I throw in an onion, salt and pepper, and Accent, and let them keep on boiling. Like

Mama, when the water starts to get a little low again, I peel some white potatoes and throw them in there. As soon as the potatoes are done, you have practically a whole meal in there. If you want, you can throw in some green peas and have the whole meal right in 1 pot.

A variation of this involves using the roast pan in the oven instead of using a pot on top of the stove. If you're not in a position to keep watching the pot to keep it from boiling over, then the oven can be very handy. I turn mine to about 350° and put everything in there, including the water and the vegetables. Then I don't have to worry about a thing. Toward the end, if I want to reduce the amount of juice, I simply remove the top and let the whole business cook down a little bit. Sometimes I use a flour-and-water thickening for the gravy. However you cook pork, it's best if you cook it a long time. I think that pork is at its best when it is practically falling off the bone.

My good friend Julia Mae is one of the finest cooks I've ever met. Her mother, Edwina, was like a second mother to me. Julia Mae was head dietician for years at a prominent place in Chicago.

BRAISED SHORT RIBS WITH TACOS AND NOODLES (Julia Mae Roberts)

The ingredients are 4 short ribs (if you have a large family, naturally you'll have to use more), 1 package of taco seasoning, 2 onions, 1 large can of tomatoes, and 1 large can of tomato sauce.

Heat some oil in a large skillet, roll the ribs in flour that has been seasoned with salt and pepper. Brown the ribs in the skillet on both sides. Put the ribs into a roasting pan and sprinkle diced onion over them. Mix in the can of tomatoes, the tomato sauce, and taco seasoning. Cover the pot and simmer until tender. Serve with hot buttered noodles.

SPARERIBS SUCCOTASH
(Julia Mae Roberts)

Use small spareribs for this one. Cut them into
pieces. Cover them with water and let them simmer until they are almost done, then add fresh or
frozen lima beans and cook them until tender. Now
add whole-kernel corn and fresh tomatoes (or 1
can of tomatoes). When everything gets hot, that
will be succotash. On top of the mixture, add diced
okra. Let the whole concoction simmer until the
okra is tender but firm. Thicken the mixture at last
with cornstarch, as I have told you how to do it
elsewhere in the book. Serve with corn bread. Yeah
man!

JEAN'S RIBS HEAVEN
(Jean DiMaio)

Remember Jean from Jean's Beans? The wonderful
cook, Jean DiMaio. She has a way with ribs, too.
She has the butcher semisplit the ribs just to remove
excess fat. Now there are 2 ways to precook ribs
before barbecuing them. You can hard-boil them
for 35 to 45 minutes, but I find ribs are tastier if
you take Jean's advice and sprinkle them liberally
with salt, pepper, garlic powder, paprika, then
place them in a roast pan with a small amount of
water. Cover them and bake them for 45 minutes.
By the way, roasting bags are great for this purpose.
Jean put me onto these bags, and I resisted the idea
at first. I'm an old-fashioned cook, and I thought,
Why a paper bag in my oven? It'll pop open in
there. Then I got to thinking about how good
those ribs are when she cooks them. And I decided
that if they helped her ribs to that extreme deli-
ciousness, then I was going to try the bags too.
  Remove the ribs from the oven and dribble
honey on them. Now there is a real hot word,

dribble. It takes a strange cook like Jean or me to
dribble anything in the kitchen. Place the ribs on
the barbecue and turn them when they are brown.
After you turn them, dribble honey on the other
side. As you can see, Jean is a real dribbler. When
both sides are brown, start brushing the ribs with
barbecue sauce, whatever one is your favorite. Keep
brushing and turning the ribs over the charcoal until they reach the desired crispness. Pile them on a
platter and deliver them up to your friends. Then
be prepared for plenty of messy-lipped kisses, because one by one those people are going to fall
madly in love with you. That last is advice directly
from Jean, and if she says so, it must be true.

By the way, you don't have to be able to cook
outdoors in order to make these ribs. If you don't
have access to an outdoor barbecue, or if the season
is wrong for you to cook out there, then you can do
almost as well with the oven and broiler.

It's been many years now that I've had the friendship of a wonderful woman, the Honorable Ambassador Perle Mesta. Of course, you know her as
the hostess with the mostess on the ball. You may
not realize that she is a former ambassador to
Luxembourg. As I write this, I have just talked with
her by phone as she recuperates from an accident
in which she broke her hip. I asked her if I could
do anything for her. She said, "Just pray for me,
just pray." That's some woman. When she is on
her feet and running full tilt with her many responsibilities and her parties for people in the
Washington scene, it takes a great many assistants
just to keep up with her.

Not too long ago, Mrs. Mesta gave a sit-down
dinner for me. She is letter perfect when it comes
to protocol. She has to be, because so many titled
people come to her parties. Ordinarily, it's the
senator over there and the ambassadors at this table,
and so forth. When she sat me at this dinner, she
broke protocol. She put me and the late Senator
Ellender at a table with the ambassadors. Senator

Ellender, who was head of the Southern bloc, turned out to be a terrific man with conversation. He and I had a wonderful talk through dinner.

Afterward, Mrs. Mesta asked me what the Senator and I talked about all that time. I told her that all the way through we talked about cooking. It turned out that Senator Ellender loved to make candy. He told me before we left that night that he was going to send me some of his candy. I sent him a copy of *Talking to Myself.*

The candy arrived beautifully wrapped in a gorgeous tin box. Inside, each separate piece was wrapped in foil. It was a kind of chocolate candy, very hard and lumpy, with nuts in it. Extraordinarily good! I enjoyed the Senator, a likable man. If he were alive, I would jot a note to remind him of our visit. I'd ask for the recipe too. He would be pleased.

APRICOT SOUFFLÉ
(Perle Mesta)

One time Mrs. Mesta said to me, "We are the two Pearls. We don't show off, but we impress people." The food at her table is always flawless. This soufflé is *especially* good.

Wash 1 pound of dried apricots, add 4 cups water, simmer for 35 minutes. *Add* 1½ cups of sugar, and boil 5 minutes longer. Put through a ricer (there should be 1 cup of pulp). Whip until foamy 5 egg whites together with ⅛ teaspoon salt. Add ¼ teaspoon cream of tartar, and continue to whip egg whites until stiff. Fold in apricot pulp and, if desired, ½ cup broken nut meats and 1 teaspoon grated lemon rind.

Place soufflé in a 9″ baking dish. Set in pan of hot water and bake at 275° for one hour.

Serve hot or cold with a sauce made of the following ingredients: 2 eggs, separated, 1 cup of confectioner's sugar, 1½ teaspoons vanilla (or 2 tablespoons brandy or sherry), ½ pint whipping cream.

Beat egg yolks, add sugar gradually, and beat. Add vanilla, brandy, or sherry. Whip cream and fold into mixture. Whip egg whites until stiff and fold in.

PECAN COOKIES
(Perle Mesta)

Ingredients: 1 cup brown sugar, 2 teaspoons granulated sugar, 3 sticks butter, 2½ cups flour, 2 teaspoons buttermilk, 3 packages pecans, ½ teaspoon baking soda, spices to taste (ginger, cinnamon, nutmeg).

Cream sugar and butter together. Add remaining ingredients and drop desired size onto greased cookie sheet. Bake in 375° oven for 10 to 15 minutes.

PENNY'S FAVORITE
BLINTZES
(Penelope Ann Adams)

My trips to Washington often include visits to both Mrs. Mesta and the White House. After all, President Nixon *has* appointed *me* an ambassador too—"Ambassador of Love to the Whole World."

Penelope Ann Adams works in the White House. She is the wonderful young lady who always helps to make arrangements for my visits there. I have developed a special friendship with her, and so I felt I could ask her for a favorite recipe. This one is Penny's own, and it sounds so good that I think they should try it at the White House dinners.

Ingredients: 2 eggs, 1 cup milk, 1 cup sifted flour, 1 teaspoon salt, ½ pound cottage cheese, sugar and cinnamon to taste, 1 egg, grated rind of 1 orange, butter, sour cream.

Beat 2 eggs thoroughly in a small bowl and add to them alternately 1 cup of milk and 1 cup of sifted flour (with a teaspoon of salt in it). Keep stirring as these things are added and until the batter is smooth.

Heat a small iron frying pan about 6" in diameter and butter it lightly with a pastry brush or a piece of soft cloth.

Pour in about 2 tablespoons of batter, or enough just to cover the bottom of the pan, tipping the pan quickly with a circular motion. Hold the pan over the flame for about 30 seconds, or until the pancake is dry. Cook it on 1 side only and shake it out onto a damp towel. Repeat this process, first reheating the pan thoroughly so that it will cook the next cake. When all the batter has been used, roll the pancakes in the damp towel until you are ready to fill and fry them.

For the filling, mash ½ pound of cottage cheese with a little sugar and cinnamon. Beat in 1 egg and the grated rind of the orange. Place 1 tablespoon of the filling in the center of each pancake and roll it up.

Fry the blintzes in hot melted butter, turning them to heat and brown on all sides. Serve with sour cream.

VEAL CHOPS GRANDE
(Julia Mae Roberts)

I want you to have a few more of Julia Mae's best. This one is well named, because it refers to the great or large taste, and that's exactly what you get. Get enough veal chops to suit your family. Also, you will need salt, pepper, oregano, 3 cups of frozen or canned lima beans, some sliced onions, chicken soup or chicken-bouillon cubes, and a bit of flour.

Sprinkle the chops with flour. Salt and pepper them to taste. Put the beans and onions in a pan with 1 stick of butter and some water. (Some would use milk, but hell, you have paid enough for the chops!) Now throw in the bouillon cube and the chops. Cover the skillet and simmer for 30 minutes over moderate flame. I suggest that with this you have a nice plain salad, and some buttered rice.

KIDNEY BEANS
WITH SAUSAGE BALL
AND RICE
(Julia Mae Roberts)

The ingredients are 1 pound of kidney beans, 2 green peppers, 2 red onions, 1 clove of garlic, 1 pound of sausage meat (hot or mild), salt and pepper. Chop up the peppers, onions, and garlic. Put the beans in enough water to cover them and then some. More water than beans, you understand? Add the chopped onions, pepper, and garlic, and let that mixture simmer until the beans are almost done. While you're waiting for that, make balls of sausage meat, about the size of cherry tomatoes, those little teeny-weeny tomatoes. Drop these balls in with the beans and let the pot simmer until the sausage is done. This is particularly good if you pour that whole thing over hot steaming rice, as Julia does.

MEAT AND VEGETABLE
MINESTRONE

Pour a little oil into a large pot. Cook about 6 pounds of hamburger with garlic, onion, 1 can of tomatoes, parsley, salt, and pepper. Let it simmer for a while, then fill the pot ¾ full of water and add 3 or 4 boxes of mixed vegetables (one leafy, at least). Cover and cook 45 minutes to 1 hour, boiling all the way.

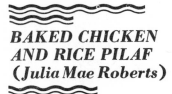

BAKED CHICKEN
AND RICE PILAF
(Julia Mae Roberts)

This one is a little more on the complicated side, because the chicken and the rice and the sauce all require some pretty special attention. If you like a challenge, try it sometime.

Start with a fryer cut in quarters. Season it with garlic, salt, and pepper. Put it in a baking dish, skin side down, and pour melted butter over it. Bake the chicken until it is tender, turning it over once during the process.

Now for the rice pilaf. Besides rice, the contents are 6 strips of bacon, 2 onions, 2 tablespoons of parsley, 1 can of mushroom pieces, 1 tablespoon of ground oregano, and 1 can of chicken broth. Fry the bacon crisp ahead of time. When you're ready to prepare the rice, sauté the onions, diced, until they are transparent. Now add all the other extras and the cooked rice.

Now, of course, you're ready to make the sauce. You will make the drippings from the chicken into a kind of gravy by adding flour and cooking it until it is just golden. As you do this, add water or chicken broth, stirring constantly until the mixture reaches the desired thickness. Let it simmer slowly for a few minutes.

When you're ready to serve the plates, crumble the bacon into the rice and put the rice on the plate first. Then the chicken goes on top of that and the sauce goes over everything. That ought to be good enough for anybody.

ITALIAN MOSTACCIOLI NOODLE CASSEROLE (Julia Mae Roberts)

Get 2 large onions, 2 green peppers, 2 stalks of celery, 2 cloves of garlic. Chop them and sauté them together until they are soft. In a skillet, sauté hamburger until crumbly and firm. Then mix the hamburger with the vegetables and add 2 large cans of tomato sauce, 1½ teaspoons of oregano, and 1 teaspoon of basil. Let this simmer for 1 hour and it will turn into a delicious meat sauce. While that is simmering, cook the noodles. When the noodles and the meat sauce are both ready, you are going to turn into a builder. Line the bottom of the baking dish with meat sauce, then put a layer of noodles over that and sprinkle with grated sharp cheese. Repeat this stacking process until you run out of ingredients or until you approach the top of the dish. Let it cook in a 350° oven for 45 minutes. Serve with garlic bread and a salad of tomatoes and cucumbers. Wow! Wow! Wow!

ROLLED APPLE PANCAKES
(Julia Mae Roberts)

Just the title of this one turns me on. Ingredients are 3 eggs, ½ cup of water, ½ cup of milk, 3 tablespoons of melted butter, 2½ cups of flour, 3 tablespoons of sugar, and a pinch of salt. Mix all of this well and make pancakes light brown.

Now get some canned apples of the sort that are sold for pie filling. Add sugar to taste, and some raisins and cinnamon. When you have this thoroughly mixed, put a spoonful of it in the corner of a pancake and roll to the other side. In other words, you are wrapping the apple mixture in a kind of pancake blanket. Line these up in a baking dish or a pan and pour melted butter over the little packages. Slip the pan into the oven and cook it until the pancakes are bubbly. Serve with the topping of powdered sugar or sour cream.

One of my favorite people in the world recently took an indefinite leave of absence from all the people who love him very much. I'm talking about Gil Hodges, the late manager of the New York Mets baseball team. Before that, he was one of the greatest first basemen who ever lived, and always a beautiful human being. He had a wonderful family, Joanie and four lovely children. Joanie and I remain very close friends. After Gil's passing, she said to me, "I don't think you know how much my husband really loved you." She had called me from

Florida where she was staying with her son Gilly, who is also now a ballplayer in the minors. I said, "Joanie, yes I do." I knew that Gil loved me in friendship because he and Joanie were calling every other day when they heard I was sick in the hospital. It actually was a heavy concern to Gil Hodges that I wasn't up to par. That could be because one time Gil had a minor heart attack; he knew what heart trouble was about.

It pleases me to think back over the wonderful times that he and Joanie and I have had. In 1965, at the Americana Hotel in New York, Gil gave me his first baseball shirt from the Dodgers—Number 14. I know that number is going into the Hall of Fame one of these days. Of course, I have been an avid Mets fan all along. I even think of myself as a front-row mascot for the team. It's been a little harder for me to go to the ball games, knowing that I won't see Number 14 trot out there. I used to sit there in the box with Joanie, and now she's not going either. If I go by myself, I'm lonely both ways.

When I started out in *Hello, Dolly!* I had a fairly small apartment with a practically nothing kitchenette in it. Gil and Joanie were worried that maybe I wasn't eating properly. Actually, I was cooking what I needed, and was doing fine. Darling Mickey, the girl who helped me so much during that period, was still alive then, and she was helping me prepare some food. Mickey's life and death—I have told that story in *Talking to Myself.* Anyway, about every other day I would hear a knock at the door and there would be Gilly, Jr., all 6'1", about eighteen years old, with some kind of big pot full of lasagna or something. Joanie kept sending food over to me. You never forget a thing like that. Once or twice, they sent so much food that I didn't even have any place to *put* it in my kitchen, and I couldn't have *eaten* it all in a hundred years. I turned to Mickey once and said, "I guess Joanie must think I'm entertaining the whole Mets team up here."

Now I'm going to give you some of Joanie's

recipes. But there's a warning that goes with that. When she says something will serve 4 to 6 people, she really means if you don't have an eater like Gil Hodges was. That man could put away four servings by himself. He was 6'2" tall and weighed 200 pounds. He wasn't a fat man, but he had a large stature.

CHICKEN À LA CALABRASE
(*Joanie Hodges*)

The ingredients are as follows: 1 chicken, cut up, ½ cup Wesson oil, 1 teaspoon of salt, 1 teaspoon of pepper, 1 whole onion (large), 1 teaspoon of basil leaf, ½ glass (juice size) of red wine, 1 half cup of water, 1 can tomato *sauce,* 1 can tomato *paste.*

Warm the oil in a skillet. Add the chicken. When the chicken starts to brown, add the whole sliced onion. Next add all spices and put on the cover. Let it steam for about 10 minutes. Then add ½ can of tomato paste and 1 whole can of tomato sauce (medium size), and ½ can of water. Cover again and let it steam until the chicken is done. Stir occasionally. This will serve 4 to 6 people. Serve with a green vegetable and a salad.

LINGUINI WITH TOASTED
FLAVORED BREAD CRUMBS
(*Joanie Hodges*)

Ingredients: ½ cup Wesson oil, 2 cloves garlic, 1 whole cup flavored bread crumbs, ¼ cup grated Italian cheese, 1½ cups water, 1 tablespoon parsley, 1 pound linguini.

Into a frying pan, put the bread crumbs, grated cheese, and parsley. Toast slowly over a low flame, gradually stirring the bread crumbs. After they are toasted, remove them from the skillet. Now add ½ cup of oil to the skillet. Put in the garlic and

brown it slowly. Remove the garlic from the oil
and let the oil cool. Add the water to the oil.

Cook the linguini in a separate pot and drain it.
Stir the seasoned bread crumbs all through the
linguini. Finally, add the other ingredients and
mix once more. This is delicious with a salad.

I've told you about cooking for my variety-show
tapings at the Hollywood Palace. I did a similar
thing on a Flip Wilson show, where I appeared as a
guest. I decided to cook the food that Flip and I
were going to eat during the taping for a certain
scene. I knew the producer would have catered food
brought in, but I told him *I* would cook something.
I got home and threw four chickens into the oven
to bake. I took them out before bed, and when I
got up the next morning I went for a swim and
crocheted part of a shawl, then fixed macaroni and
cheese. Oh yes, I also cooked the simplest vegetable
of all, green peas with butter and sugar. That butter
and sugar is a real secret weapon. Everything was
just delicious; it was a fattening TV show. Flip is a
deep and sensitive man. I felt a special rapport with
him and I'm proud to have him as a friend.

On the other hand, you know, things can work
the other way too. Sometimes the *food* in the world
of show business can be as lavish and fancy as all
the *rest* of that world. For a lady of simple style,
like me, that can sometimes be a bit confusing. For
example, I remember meeting Otto Preminger
when I was entertaining in London. He said he
was going to a special dinner in England and asked
me to go along with him. We went to the home of
a famous producer.

It was apparent from the beginning that we were
going to do some fairly fancy eating. I could see it
coming. It was going to be the *Queen Mary* all over
again. I started to get a little nervous, and actually
inhaled a couple of cigarettes, and then I didn't
even know how to smoke. Well, the reason I was
doing all of this serious smoking, if I'm going to tell
the truth, is that the lady put in front of me what I

thought was a very strange thing. It was an artichoke. I knew the name of it, but I had no idea how to eat it. It was sitting up all nice and green, and looked to me like a small palm tree without the trunk. There was some cream around it. I just sat there and looked. I went through four cigarettes waiting for somebody to make a move toward that thing. I simply had to see what they were going to do with it. I did what they did, but I couldn't taste a thing because I had smoked so many cigarettes while I was waiting. I guess I'll just have to try artichoke again sometime under better circumstances.

Epilogue

N 1934 I was appearing on Broadway in a wonderful play called *House of Flowers*. For days I knew that I wasn't feeling well, and I suspected that something was wrong. I could walk down the street and just fall down for no good reason that I knew of. There was a weakness, a complete loss of energy. Any kind of play, when you appear in it every night, requires a lot of stamina. At first I thought that maybe I was just tired from all the performances. I was determined not to miss a single night of the play, so I kept pushing on. As it turned out later, I found out that I was suffering from a combination of extreme fatigue and anemia. Next door to the theater was a good Spanish restaurant called, I think, Fornos. They heard over there that I was having a little trouble and one day they prepared a mixture for me that I'll never forget. It was liver. *Raw* liver, mind you, ground up, with a little salt added. They put that ground liver in a cup and told me to eat it if I wanted to feel better. Well, looking at it, I wasn't sure I *wanted* to feel better, but I decided to give it a try. Of course, you know that looking at that raw liver made my imagination run pretty fast. Nevertheless, I ate every bite, under protest. It pulled me out of trouble, but it made me decide that liver was out for a while, maybe even a *long* while. Then, a few years later, in London of all places (where roast beef reigns supreme), I discovered that calf liver can be utterly delicious. I was appearing nightly at The Talk of the Town, and afterward each night I would go to The Colony Club to have a bite to eat. Because I went there regularly, Hettie and Alf, the proprietors of the club, became very close friends of mine. One night I couldn't decide what to eat. Hettie advised calf liver. I hesitated, trying to find a polite way to decline, but she persisted. Finally, I said, "Okey-doke, Honey, let's try the liver." That liver was so good that I ordered it every single night during the remainder of my stay there.

Toward the end of my visit I had decided that I had to get that recipe. But I knew that it wasn't always polite to ask the chef for a prized recipe. I sent so many messages of praise back to the kitchen that the chef finally had to come out and take a bow. As a matter of fact, he took three. Count on a vaudevillian to be counting! Then he paid me the supreme compliment of giving me his recipe. It's so simple you won't believe it. Are you ready?

COLONY CLUB LIVER SUPREME

To start with, cut up lots of onions. I mean *lots,* because I really dig onions. I put them in a skillet with about a stick of butter or more and let them simmer slowly, covered, over a low flame. Be sure to turn the fire way down so that you won't burn them. Wash the liver thoroughly, sprinkle with salt, pepper, and flour, and drop it into the pan right on top of the onions. I suppose that when you do it you will take the time to lay each piece of liver in there very carefully and neatly. I don't do it that way because I'm a queer kind of cook. I just pile it in. Then I keep turning it over and moving it around now and then until each piece starts to look a little brown. Be careful now, you don't want shoe leather, so don't cook it too long. Bring it to the point where it is just done enough for your family and then stop cooking. In my house, Louis likes his liver a little soft and medium, so I take his out first and let the rest of it get just a bit more firm.

Now isn't that simple? I guess most of us have always tried to serve liver once in a while just because we know it's so good for you. I can promise you that if you start cooking liver just this way, you will never again feel that you have to apologize for serving calf liver.

As you must know by now, I get a lot of pleasure out of finding something new and groovy to cook, something that I never knew I liked. Still, I must keep my hand in with the old standards, things like chicken-in-the-pot or a good pot of lima beans. These basic things are hard to beat in the long run. I find that when I want to take food to someone's house, just to show that I'm thinking of them, I always resort to the oldest tried and true recipes.

The other day, for example, I called to Dee Dee, "Why don't you go call Mr. Parvin for me. He's on my mind for some reason." I sometimes feel that I am a kind of fortune teller. I get "radiations" about people and I find it's a good thing to follow up on those feelings. She came back and said, "Mr. Parvin is fine." Then I said, "Well then, I'm going to get up and put on a pot of beans for him. I feel like I should, because if he's all right then I guess he came to my mind because it's time to send him another pot of beans." I send Mr. Parvin a pot of beans, those good fat lima beans, about three or four times a year. At Christmas he gets the biggest pot of beans, and at other times he gets the smaller ones. In fact, Mr. Parvin likes my beans so much that I can't see lima beans without thinking about that nice man.

I do the same sort of thing when I hear that some friend of mine is not feeling well. I'm not for barging in on people, because I really don't like to have people drop in on me, especially if I'm not feeling well. What I do instead is to cook chicken-in-the-pot. Then I get in the car with that pot of chicken while it's still hot (sometimes I don't even have shoes on). I'll drive over to the house and just leave it. Whoever answers the door, I just hand it in with the potholders and say that I'm on my way. That's my way of visiting when things are a little rough. I don't do that necessarily because I think the people need some food to eat. I do it the same way for people I know who have seventeen servants and eighteen freezers full of food. I do it because it's my way of saying I love them and I'm thinking about them.

Mr. Parvin never fails to call up and say how good the beans were. As a matter of fact, when he built a new home he put a kitchen in it that was a real showplace. If the truth were known, he probably doesn't need such a fancy kitchen, but the reason he gave was that Pearlie Mae was going to come over there and cook a pot of beans once in a while. I suppose one day I'll have to try that.

Blah food is a drag. I think that food should be salted during the cooking, because if you get to the table and have to salt every bite you're going to have too much salt and it isn't really going to get *into* the food anyway. No one who comes to my tables reaches for the salt before he tastes the food, because I do a pretty good job of putting that salt in there at the stove. Most restaurant food needs salt, because I suppose they prepare in large quantities and they have to think about people who can't handle salt because of heart and other ailments.

Of course, I know that too much salt is not really good for you. When I had to check into the hospital with heart trouble, one of the first things they did was to take me completely off salt. Just trying to do without it practically gave me another heart attack. I thought it was the end of all eating. I noticed an interesting thing, though—a lot of weight fell off me right away. Part of it was that I wasn't eating very much, and the rest was that the salt wasn't making me hold water in my system.

I was about to go crazy because I missed salt so much, when another patient told me about "diet salt." Well, I mentioned it to my doctor and he said I could use it. Of course, you know it wasn't salt at all. I got all excited anyway. I was beginning to think I was ready to stay in the hospital for a year if necessary, if I could just have the salt. That night when they brought my dinner I really laid that stuff on top. It looked pretty good sprinkling out there, and I know that the delight showed on my face as I lifted that first bite to my lips. Well, after that first bite all I wanted to do was go back to sleep. Let it be recorded here that there really isn't any decent substitute for salt. That diet salt tasted exactly like *lead!*

The way I love salt you would think that I would drink a lot of water. Actually, I don't drink twelve glasses of water a year. I don't know why, I just don't want it. My husband, Louis, can consume from two to eight pitchers of water a day. Of course, a drummer burns up lots of energy, and he can get pretty dry with the perspiration and all. But it seems to me that Louis *thrives* on water. He drops a lot of weight during a performance. I suppose if they thought it would work, every heavy woman in America would take up drums. Louis is not a large man, but he can lose as much as four pounds during a single performance.

I think a lot of women are deeply concerned about recovering that figure that their husbands liked so much, that figure they had when they first got married—the slim waistline and the flat tummy, and so forth. A lot of women just don't understand why their weight can fluctuate so much. I mean these are the diet-conscious people that I'm talking about. A lot of that fluctuation has to do with water. There are times when we can simply pop up with extra weight, a lot of which is pure water. I asked my doctor about this one time, and he told me something that I've since found out is true. What bothered me was that I had gained about five pounds in only a few days, and I didn't know why. The fact is that some women accumulate water in their systems during a menstrual period. Another thing that can make me get puffy is to get very, very tired. Real fatigue can cause some people to puff up and retain water. I actually swell physically when I get very tired. On the other hand, I find that when I get proper basic rest, and for me six hours may be enough, I become an altogether different person. If I can get on that kitchen floor sometimes (or any floor) and stretch out and just go right to sleep, I get up and my entire body tone is different and better. My body seems to relax, release fluids, and to put itself in shape again. When I wake up in the morning after a really good night's rest I think I'm beautiful. I look in that mirror and I can see the change. My figure is divine!

Well, what do I consume if I don't like water? Come to think of it, I consume quite a bit of juice and coffee. On days when I find myself drinking lots of coffee, I feel like an awkward balloon at the end of the day. Here's another thing about coffee that can put a little weight on you—sugar. I don't use it. I've never been a great sugar user. I used to put cream in there, and that may be worse than anything. I think I got in the habit of putting cream in my coffee when I was traveling around to so many bad restaurants. Bad, burnt coffee may turn all sorts of sickening colors, but you can drink it if you get enough cream in it. Lately, I've turned back to straight black coffee with a little sugar substitute added.

I've had a few things to say in here about fatigue and strain and heart difficulties. I want to be sure that I tell you that food is not the *whole* answer. Sometimes emotional things can cause weariness in a way that physical things don't make you tired. I think it was in about 1966 that I discovered something about emotionality in myself. I was in England and I had to go to Mr. Foster's office at the Foster Agency. In the course of discussing business, we had some kind of disagreement that upset me a bit. Frankly, I don't remember exactly what it was. I moved toward the door of the office and started down the long hall toward the street. Mr. Foster came to the door and called after me, "Pearl, now don't run away and be angry." I remember turning to him, and at that moment, the truth dawned on me. I said, "Mr. Foster, I'm not running and I'm not angry. I'm walking away so I can walk back later."

Ever since that time, I have been trying to live that way. You see, all my young life I could get hurt and angry and worried. When that happened to me the stress was enormous. I would stay and do battle, or else I would run away emotional and angry. Maybe the measured pace comes with a little maturity. But I have found that it saves me time and again. I just walk away from a bad situation sometimes, and I feel that there is a certain strength in that. Putting up your dukes can only lead to trouble, and sometimes you can't repair what you've done. Sometimes, in fact, you can't so easily forgive what someone *else* has done. If you identify the right moment to walk away from a situation, the chances are much better that you can come back later with a smile on your face and deal with things calmly and evenly.

Now I'm starting to sound like an old philosopher, but I guess that's honest, because there is some of that in me. Anyway, I'm going to pass along another little piece of advice related to the first one. Sometimes you have to make *good use* of *trouble*. You have to find the beauty in ugliness, or it will defeat you. In March of 1966 I finished a concert at Philharmonic Hall in New York. Tony Fantozzi, my friend and agent, came backstage. It had been one of those wonderful times when the audience had responded to everything, and there was a sense of elation afterward. Tony was trying to sum up the whole evening and to tell me how delighted he was. Actually, the thing that gave us the most pleasure was that in that concert I had been able to overcome all kinds of difficulties that had occurred, even in that fine hall. We had had a full house. The place was packed with hip and intelligent people. That puts the pressure on a performer in the first

place. Right away, the sound system had started
acting up. Then there was some kind of bug in the
lighting system. Also a piece of property had been
put in the wrong place and it was in my way when
I tried to perform. All these things together could
have demolished some performers. It could have
shattered their program and destroyed their concen-
tration. What gave me a special pride was that every
time something went wrong, I ad-libbed my way
out of it and turned the whole thing to my own
good advantage. The audience loved it. That kind
of experience causes you to grow, and it gives you
a confidence that you can't get in any other way.

Stage people often try to rehearse me pretty heavily for the opening of a new show, or for a special
concert. I refuse to do it. If there are any surprises
out there for me, I would just as soon meet them
during the performance itself and take my chances
on making a good thing out of any difficulties that
might arise. I feel the same way about living offstage. People generally fear the accident, the unex-
pected. Most performers, I think, are scared to death
that something will go wrong with a carefully
orchestrated program. My own observation is that
audiences really thrive on spontaneity. A little flaw
here and there, if you turn it around to your advantage, only endears you to the audience more
than ever.

When I have one of those wonderful evenings
when nothing has been able to shake me or hold
me back, and when the audience responds fully, I
have to stand there in the applause at the end of the
performance and lower my head. A kind of wonder
overtakes me. It is an awe mixed with gratitude.
I ask myself, "What could I have done to make
these people respond this way, and how am I going
to thank them? What words can come out of my
mouth at this moment?" I find that I usually say
the same thing: "I have given to you only what
God has given to me, and that I give freely. You
see, folks, I never work on the stage, I have *fun*
up here. And why *not?* That is what makes the

whole thing worth it." I could boil it down this way—when you can give of yourself freely and fully, humanity forgets to pick you apart. Then you are on your way.

Giving from the stage and giving from the kitchen are all part of the same impulse for me. I have told you about my experiences with hungry children in England after the war. To this day, I cannot bear the thought of anyone, young or old, starving for the lack of food. I may as well get this off my mind and say it as clearly as I can. It has to do with *surplus foods.*

In 1953 I enjoyed a trip to Germany, and I loved the simple German cooking. I was struck by a neatness and a kind of efficiency in the German approach to food. It carried right over into the way they *grow* their food. They didn't have a great surplus of land for growing things, but it seemed to me that they had made full use of every single square inch of available farmland. There was enough to go around because they managed it so well.

As far as food is concerned, the Germans seemed to recover from the war as fast or faster than anyone else. When I was there I had a steak which was as thick as my head, and that is pretty thick. It made me think of that miserable little excuse for a steak that I had been served in England only a few short years before. The Germans had Maxwell House coffee and all manner of good things to eat. Of course, I'm sure that it made a difference that we had our armies over there and *they* had to be supplied. But, Honey, that food was *there.*

The United States produces enormous quantities of food. In fact, we often hear about the surpluses of foods in this country. From time to time this nation sends surplus wheat, surplus rice, surplus this and that to other places in the world. Now you know that I'm basically a person with an impulse to give, to nourish, to sustain, to satisfy needs in others. I say that because I don't want to be misinterpreted in what I am going to say next. It just seems absolutely obvious to me that this country does not have any surplus food as long as we have hungry people in America. There is no surplus, is there, really? I cannot understand how we can put together all those programs for sending food across the oceans when at home we have people who are slowly starving to death. We could use less foreign aid and more home aid. Can it be that this nation is using food as a kind of barter, a kind of exchange for something in the way of loyalty? If that is true, it makes the problem even worse, in my view. Hungry people cannot be good at learning or producing anything, except perhaps violence. We ought to be concerned about that in this country first, and then decide whether we have anything we would call a surplus. President Hoover talked about a chicken in every pot. I say that you don't necessarily have to have a *chicken* in there, but for God's sake we ought to be putting *something* in everybody's pot.

Well, I have a feeling that I'm coming to the end of this book. I am finishing it just as I began it, sitting in the kitchen alone in the silence of the late evening. Louis and the children are asleep at the other end of the house. I know the dogs are still up and walking around near the back door, because I hear those little tags jingling once in a while. I don't have anything on the stove, but I'm thinking about it.

As I look back over the book, I don't really know whether it is mainly a book about cooking food, or mainly a book about cooking *life*. I do know that when I sit in this room, in this chair, at this table, I can savor almost to the point of tasting the memory of a wonderful day. Or sitting here on occasion able to sit and burn out loneliness.

In a few minutes, before the dogs go to sleep, I'm going to get up and find them a little something for their late-night treat. I know that's why they're still awake. Maybe a dab of peanut butter on a piece of paper. Sometimes they'll get leftovers. One night last week I looked around in the icebox and found that I had some cabbage and some rice. Those guys never had it so good. I stepped out the back door before bed and put down a plate of steamed cabbage and buttered rice. It is my pleasure, a kind of nightly ritual.

Once I have done that, I think that I will come back and put some kind of pan on the stove. I don't know just yet what I'm going to cook, but I'm going to do it with images of my family in my mind's eye. I'm going to bring a good day to an end by going to the stove and preparing something tonight, so that tomorrow I can put something maybe a little special on the table. I must think of something that I haven't done for a while. When I put it before them tomorrow, I will do so with the same spirit that I feel in bringing this book to you. I put these pages before you with love, with all the great love, from Pearl.

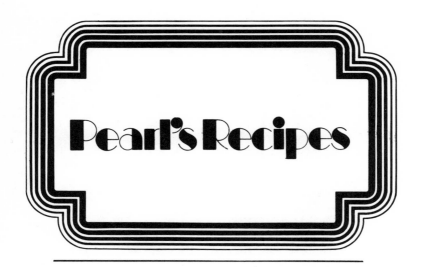

Pearl's Recipes